Understanding Scientology: The Demon Cult

Understanding Scientology: The Demon Cult

Margery Wakefield

DEDICATION

Have nothing to do with the fruitless
deeds of darkness, but rather
expose them.
Ephesians 5:11

This book is dedicated to all victims of the destructive
cult of Scientology.

L. RON HUBBARD ON SCIENTOLOGY

"In all the broad universe there is no other hope for man than ourselves." *Ron's Journal 67*

"We're playing for blood, the stake is EARTH." *HCO Policy Letter 7, November, 1962*

"Scientology is the most vital movement on Earth today." *The Aims of Scientology*

"We are the FREE People. We LIVE! We're free." *We Are the Free People*

"Scientology is the only workable system Man has." *Safeguarding Technology*

"We're the elite of Planet Earth." *The Eighteenth ACC*

"We're free men and women—probably the last free men and women on Earth." *Your Post*

"We are the first group on earth that knew what they were talking about. All right, sail in. The world's ours. Own it." *The World Is Ours*

"Auditors have since the first session of Scientology been the only individuals on this planet in this universe capable of freeing Man." *Auditors*

"The whole agonized future
of this planet, every Man,
Woman, and Child on it, and
your own destiny for the next
endless trillions of years depends
on what you do here and now
with and in Scientology." *Keeping
Scientology Working*

EX-MEMBERS ON SCIENTOLOGY

"Earth would be better off without them." PF

"Frankly, I'm disgusted by the whole thing, ashamed I was ever involved with it, and I wish the entire organization would fall off the face of the earth." SD

"I feel that I have been damaged. I feel that I have been robbed. I feel that Scientology has done more family damage than anything else I can think of." LD

"The Church of Scientology is a serious menace to society, and every effort should be made to bring out the truth about it to the public." JB

"The Church of Scientology caused much damage to me. Some can't be repaired." TP

"I still have nightmares." KR

"Scientology is a destructive group that gradually alienates people from their family, friends, and their society. This is a group to stay away from at all cost." CB

"They're a bunch of money-grubbing nuts." MF

"It embodies some of the ugliest of human qualities: arrogance, self-righteousness, self-deception, prejudice, and stupidity." SH

"The Church of Scientology is a krock [sic] of shit." RK

"I'm glad to be out of it." RF

CONTENTS

The use of *he* as pronoun
for nouns embracing both
genders is a simple, practical
convention rooted in the
beginnings of the English
language. It has no pejorative
connotation; it is never incorrect.

Strunk and White,
Elements of Style, Third Edition,
1979

PREFACE

Late on a warm summer evening, I returned to my apartment from the local university. I had spent the evening there, as I frequently did, practicing on one of the pianos at the music school. I felt calm and peaceful—a brief reprieve from the chaos of recent events in my life.

My mood changed quickly, as I approached my small apartment and found the door wide open. *That's impossible,* I thought. *I always lock the door when I leave.*

Having one's life threatened periodically tends to make one less careless about details like locking the door.

The apartment was clearly empty, so I looked for evidence of a burglary. I was puzzled when I found the living room, kitchen, and bathroom all normal. Everything was as I left it a few hours earlier.

Then I walked into the bedroom and froze in horror. On the far wall, by the bed, a dark-red liquid had been splashed against the wall and dripped slowly toward the floor.

It was blood.

The message was clear. One thought formed in my mind, pushing aside all others. *Scientology.* It had to be.

For twelve years, I lived in the strange and bizarre world of Scientology. When, at the end of those twelve years, I began to question some of their practices, I was summarily offloaded, excommunicated from the cult. It would seem that the nightmare had ended, but, in fact, it had just begun.

A year-and-a-half after being expelled from Scientology, I began to realize what happened to me—that for twelve years, I'd been hypnotized and brainwashed without my knowledge or consent. I decided to sue the cult. That was when I learned the truth behind the smiling faces of Scientology.

I contacted a lawyer who was known to oppose Scientology and told him I wanted to sue. I planned to travel to see him two days later.

The following day, as I packed for my trip, someone knocked on my door. I opened it to find three Scientologists from Flag, the organizational headquarters of Scientology located in Clearwater, Florida—3,000 miles away. Somehow, they knew about my call to the lawyer.

I was taken to a motel a few miles away, and, for three days, I was psychologically "worked on" by the Scientologists. They said I was to withdraw my lawsuit, or "something could happen to me."

"You mean you'd kill me?" I asked, knowing the answer.

"It would just be a smart thing to do," they replied.

After arguing and resisting for three days, I gave in and signed their agreement, promising not to sue. I wanted to live. Finally, they left.

After four months, I contacted another lawyer and told him what had happened. "Come to Florida," he advised. "You can still sue them. That document isn't valid."

I moved to Florida and filed a civil lawsuit against the Church of Scientology. The threats began almost immediately. Scientologists in uniform came to my apartment and stood in the yard, making threats. When they learned I worked in a nearby mall, they intercepted me as I left work, threatening me if I didn't drop the lawsuit. They called my boss, asking when I'd leave work and which exit I would use.

I received phone calls in the middle of the night. Sometimes, they mentioned the names of my nieces and nephews. Shortly afterward, those relatives received mail from Scientology. Again, the message was clear.

In the morning, I found my car had flat tires, or the doors had been deeply scratched. Ten years later, I still receive calls.

When I called the police, they said, "There's nothing we can do. No crime has been committed."

No crime.

I felt like I'd been raped, first, by my experiences within the cult, then by my experiences outside it, but psychological rape isn't a crime. A terror campaign against a person by a satanic cult isn't a crime.

I entered Scientology at the age of eighteen, a shy and emotionally disturbed teenager, a psychological survivor of a painfully dysfunctional family. I had little confidence or self-esteem. Within months, I was transformed into an aggressive, radical Scientologist. As a result of daily hypnotic rituals and an unending barrage of propaganda from "bulletins" and tapes, I was completely indoctrinated and fiercely dedicated to the group.

During the next twelve years, I traveled to six cities, spreading the gospel of Scientology, working in various Scientology centers at various jobs. I did volunteer work for the Guardian's Office, the notorious CIA-like branch of the "church," which deals with such things as espionage, agents, infiltration, covers, plants, intelligence, and covert activities.

As a GO volunteer, I once sat in on a meeting in which the murder of two defectors was planned. I understood that the murders were justified on the basis of the Scientology credo: *The greatest good for the greatest number of dynamics.* In other words, the ends justified the means.

I was given written policies, with full illustrations, on how to break into and enter buildings. At one point, while working for Scientology in Washington, DC, I was required to break into the nearby headquarters of the American Psychiatric Association and steal financial and membership records, which I did.

I was coached to perjure myself in a lawsuit involving a Florida judge, and, although I never appeared in court, I was fully prepared to implicate the judge in sexual misconduct in order to serve the "church."

After a few months of a systematic program of hypnosis and indoctrination, I operated entirely on a stimulus-response basis. I would've followed any command I was given, including murder or suicide.

I wasn't alone in that. Another ex-Scientologist wrote:

> Shortly after I returned home, Jonestown occurred, and that did it for me. I realized that if at any point LRH (L. Ron Hubbard, the founder of Scientology) had handed me a glass of poison and told me to drink it, I would have with no questions asked and no second thoughts.
>
> Affidavit of an ex-Scientologist

What is interesting to me is the reaction parents have when they find out their children are in Scientology.

Each week, I receive phone calls from parents across the country. I send them information, and they begin to read. They call with questions. Then I see their growing horror as they begin to realize what really happened to them.

Someone took their children, transformed them into unthinking, belligerent strangers, and filled them with bizarre ideas that defy any logical or rational approach.

"That's because," I explain to the parent, "your child is in a trance state—hypnotized. He can't think. Don't try to reason with him. It doesn't work."

Gradually, the parents begin to understand that their child has been psychologically kidnapped by a cult—and there's nothing they can do about it.

"But this is America!" they say. "This can't happen here. Why doesn't the government do something about it?"

I want to help them. I promise to send information and give them whatever advice I can. "Write to them," I say. "See if you can get them home for a visit. Tell them repeatedly that you love them."

I'm frustrated, because, deep in my heart, I know there isn't much I can do. The only way to get someone out of a cult like Scientology is to deprogram him, and that's illegal, because it's considered kidnapping. The fact that the child has already been kidnapped psychologically, physically, mentally, and emotionally, doesn't enter in.

There is a pattern to the parents' calls. At first, they call frequently and speak in frightened, hysterical voices. Then, as they comprehend the reality of the situation, the calls become less frequent. They're paralyzed by the legal system, which lacks precedents in the gray area of mind control.

I try to be optimistic. "Never give up hope," I tell them. "A miracle can always happen. It did for my parents. Maybe it will for you. Just don't give up."

It took me ten years to be able to write this book. I knew all along that I had to do it. If you explore a strange country and find it to be a dangerous place, and you happen to be one of the few who return alive, it becomes a moral necessity to warn others of the danger.

As trite as it might sound, if I can prevent even one person, especially a young one, from having to live through the nightmare of Scientology, then I'll feel satisfied.

Willa Appel, in *Cults of America,* writes:

> Human beings need order.
> They need a framework that can
> account for and explain
> experiences.

We are all vulnerable, and vulnerability is the opportunity exploited by all cults, especially Scientology.

The antidote is information, education, and exposure. The purpose of this book is to shine a small light into the dark, secret world of Scientology.

CHAPTER ONE

From Dianetics to Scientology—
the Evolution of a Cult

> Writing for a penny a word
> is ridiculous. If a man really
> wants to make a million dollars,
> the best way would be to start
> his own religion.
>
> L. Ron Hubbard

> Scientology is here to
> rescue you.
>
> L. Ron Hubbard

L. Ron Hubbard, founder of the curious, controversial cult of Scientology, author of swashbuckling tales of mystery and adventure, could very well have stepped larger than life from the pages of one of his own stories. Flamboyant, charismatic, messiah to thousands of adulating followers, Hubbard lived by no rules but his own. In an age of anxiety, he offered to those in his thrall the comforting certainty of simple solutions to life's problems. Yet, as weaver of the complex web of Scientology, he managed to ensnare not only others but himself.

Lafayette Ronald Hubbard began his early life as the center of attention in a large, lively extended family in Helena, Montana, which included his doting grandparents and several adoring maternal aunts. His father, Harry Ron Hubbard, after a brief and unsuccessful business career, was caught up in the surge of patriotism that affected many young men following the declaration of war in 1917 between the United States and Germany and enlisted in the Navy.

When the war ended, he reenlisted as a career Naval officer. Ron's mother, May Waterbury Hubbard, was a dutiful Navy wife who was to inherit the impossible task of bridging the gap between a military father who lived life by the rules and his brilliant, unpredictable son, to whom rules were anathema.

As a child, according to his aunts, Ron Hubbard already possessed a fecund imagination, making up games and stories for the amusement of the invariably attentive adults in his world. From the beginning he possessed a capacity for fantasy he was to carry with him throughout his life. As a schoolboy, to escape the reality of dreary algebraic equations and dry history facts, he filled the pages of his school notebooks with endless swashbuckling tales of heroic adventurers in exotic, distant lands.

In later years, he created a resumé for himself, transforming his most pathetic liabilities into assets of heroic proportions—as if the boundary between fantasy and reality became blurred, even to himself. Ironically, no fantasy life he created for himself could possibly match the colorful, improbably reality he actually lived.

"I'm possessed," he once told a friend, "of an insatiable lust for power and money."

In his greed, he would siphon the energy and assets from the lives of thousands of followers, whom he regarded with sneering contempt. Although he created the vast, complex world of Scientology, in which his followers could lose themselves for years, he didn't want to be identified with his "marks."

By the early thirties, Hubbard acquired a wife and two small children. To the horror of his conservative parents, he flunked out of college and had no acceptable skills with which to support his young family. Money was a constant, wearying problem.

He soon discovered that the colorful adventures he'd been creating in notebooks for years were actually saleable to the popular pulp-fiction magazines of that era. He started slowly, but it was soon obvious that he possessed a prolific talent in writing for such magazines, named for the inferior wood-pulp paper stock on which they were printed.

His work habits were somewhat eccentric. He was a phenomenally fast writer and worked all night to produce story after story, retiring at dawn to sleep until the afternoon. However, no matter how prolific his output, he never seemed to make enough money to support his profligate spending habits.

By the mid-forties, his literary output was declining. He was well-known and respected as a writer of adventure stories, science fiction, and westerns, but he soon realized the limits of his vocation. He would never achieve power and money by writing penny-a-word pulp adventures.

The way to make money, he began to remark to friends, is to start a religion. He once addressed a group of science-fiction writers in New Jersey with the words, "Writing for a penny a word is ridiculous. If a man really wanted to make a million dollars, the best way to do it would be to start his own religion."

In 1949, Hubbard dropped out of sight. Rumor had it he was working on something new, a book of psychology. In January, 1950, a mysterious ad appeared in *Astounding Science Fiction,* a pulp magazine edited by his friend, John Campbell, promising:

> an article on the science of
> the mind, of human thought. It is
> a totally new science called

Dianetics, and it does precisely
what a science of thought should
do. Its power is almost
unbelievable; following the
sharply defined basic laws
Dianetics sets forth, physical ills
such as ulcers, asthma, and
arthritis can be cured, as can all
other psychosomatic ills....[1]

Hubbard began experimenting with his new "science" on his friends. He had them lie on a couch, close their eyes, and follow his commands to remember certain painful memories, particularly memories of prenatal experiences in the womb.

To his surprise, Campbell found himself cured of chronic sinusitis. He told others about this remarkable new science, and a small group began to form that became the nucleus for a new organization, the Hubbard Dianetics Research Foundation in Elizabeth, New Jersey.

In May, 1950, the promised article on Dianetics was published in *Astounding Science Fiction,* outlining the basics of this new science. Shortly afterward, *Dianetics: The Modern Science of Mental Health,* was released and became a best-seller.

Hubbard wasn't modest in his claims for Dianetics.

The creation of Dianetics is
a milestone for Man comparable
to his discovery of fire and
superior to his inventions of the
wheel and the arch. The hidden
source of all psychosomatic ills
and human aberrations has been
discovered, and skills have been
developed for their invariable

---

[1] Atack, p. 148

cure. [2]

> Dianetics is an adventure. It is an exploration into terra incognito, the human mind, that vast and hitherto unknown realm half an inch back of our foreheads. You are beginning an adventure. Treat it as an adventure. And may you never be the same again. [3]

Early in the book, Hubbard introduced what he called the "clear."

> Dianetically, the optimum individual is called the "clear." One will hear much of that word, both as a noun and a verb, in this volume, so it is well to spend time here at the outset setting forth exactly what can be called a clear, the goal of Dianetic therapy.
>
> A clear can be tested for any and all psychoses, neuroses, compulsions, and repressions (all aberrations) and can be examined for any self-generated diseases referred to as psychosomatic ills. These tests confirm the clear to be entirely without such ills or aberrations.[4]

---

[2] Miller, p. 155

[3] Hubbard, *Dianetics,* p. 1

[4] Ibid, p. 12

The state of Clear, Hubbard promised, was a state of mind never before achieved by man. In fact, upon achieving Clear, a person would progress from the state of Homo Sapiens to the new, advanced state of Homo Novis.

Dianetic therapy, called auditing (to listen), turned out to be an amalgam of Freudian analysis, in which a reclining patient is encouraged to recall past traumatic experiences; abreactive therapy, in which past events are reexperienced by the patient with their accompanying emotion; General Semantics of Korzybski, in which a person learns to differentiate between subconscious experiences; and the psychoanalytic theory of Nandor Fodor, in which the influence of prenatal experiences is explored.

Dianetic theory is basically simple. According to Hubbard, all the events of our lives are stored in the mind as "mental image pictures," or memories, "filed" in "chains" by similar content. A person might have a "headache chain," or a "pain-in-the-right ankle chain."

By directing the patient, called the "preclear," (one who is not yet Clear) in Dianetics, to recall and reexperience the traumatic memories on each chain, the potential of the "somatic" of that chain to "key-in" or become restimulated in the present can be erased. The memory then becomes refiled from the subconscious or "reactive mind" of Dianetics to the conscious or "analytical mind."

The success of the "auditing session" depends on the ability of the "auditor" (the person leading the session) to maintain control over the preclear and his memories.

The complete file of all the memories of an individual going back in time is called the "time track." Hubbard claimed that when a person was audited to the point that all his subconscious, "reactive" memories were refiled in the "analytical" memory banks, he would achieve the state of Clear and would never again suffer the effects of the reactive mind, which, in Dianetics, is also referred to as the "bank."

The theory is, if a person complains of a somatic in the present, such as a headache, then an earlier memory of an experience in which there was an actual injury to the head is "in restimulation." By getting the preclear to recall all headaches progressively earlier in time until the "basic" or earliest memory on the headache chain is reached, theoretically, the headache should vanish.

That is the essence of Dianetic therapy.

At a time when the only option for people suffering from painful psychosomatic symptoms was costly, time-consuming psychoanalysis, the idea of an inexpensive, easy-to-administer lay psycotherapy caught on quickly.

Within weeks, the nascent Hubbard Dianetics Research Foundation was deluged with letters and phone calls about the new "science" of Dianetics. Letters arrived at the rate of 1,000 a week. By the end of the year, over 150,000 copies of the Dianetics book had been sold. In a glowing article in the *New York Times,* a reviewer stated dramatically that *history has become a race between Dianetics and catastrophe,*[5] echoing an idea often stated by Hubbard.

By August, there were more than 100 students enrolled for the one-month Dianetics auditing course taught by Hubbard at the Foundation. The cost was $500. In addition, one could receive personal auditing, or counseling, at the Foundation for the fee of $25 per hour.

Money was pouring into the Foundation. However, due to Hubbard's extravagant spending habits, the money disappeared just as quickly. Because of a lack of formalized accounting or administrative procedures in the Foundation, much of the money went straight into Hubbard's pockets. In the first year, one staff member estimated that the

---

[5] Miller, p. 161

Foundation took in as much as $90,000, of which about only $20,000 was accounted for. [6]

By December, 1950, five new Foundations were established in Chicago, Honolulu, New York, Washington, DC, and Los Angeles. As many as 500 small, independent Dianetics counseling groups had sprung up across the country.

Hubbard had promised that the state of Clear was attainable to anyone who successfully completed enough Dianetic auditing to eradicate the troublesome reactive mind. In August, 1950, Hubbard organized a rally at the famed Shrine Auditorium in Los Angeles, at which he promised to reveal to his enthusiastic followers the world's very first Clear.

An air of hushed excitement filled the packed auditorium. Hubbard, a consummate showman, first demonstrated some Dianetic techniques to the audience, saving his surprise revelation for the end of the program.

Finally, a shy and obviously nervous young woman appeared onstage with Hubbard and was introduced as the world's first Clear. She could, Hubbard claimed, remember every moment of her life.

The audience immediately began asking questions, such as, "What did you have for breakfast on October 3, 1942? What's on page 122 of the Dianetics book?"

Embarrassingly, she didn't know. At one point, when Hubbard had his back turned to her, she was asked what color tie he wore. She couldn't answer. A physics major in school, she was asked to name some simple physics formulas but wasn't able to remember them.

Disgusted catcalls came from the audience. One by one, people walked out. The evening was a disaster. Yet amazingly, money continued pouring into the Hubbard

---

[6] Ibid, p. 116

organizations. The Shrine Auditorium debacle did little to stem the tidal wave of interest in the supposed new science of the mind.

Toward the end of the year, however, the initial enthusiasm with Dianetics began to ebb. The American Psychological Association published a report critical of Dianetics, stating there was a need for more testing, because Dianetics lacked empirical evidence.

The flow of money into the Foundations tapered off, as the novelty of Dianetics subsided. Several early associates of Hubbard in New Jersey resigned after encountering the darker side of his personality—a definite tendency toward paranoia that would, in time, sabotage almost every significant relationship in his life.

Hubbard's personal problems also began interfering with the Dianetics movement. While still married to his first wife, he bigamously married another woman. That produced a public and embarrassing divorce scandal that was carried in newspapers across the country.

Hubbard spent money faster than the Foundation could make it. Funding his grandiose schemes and unrealistic ideas was bankrupting the organizations despite the best efforts of several dedicated followers to save them.

Also, Hubbard encouraged the exploration of past lives in auditing. That, and the lack of the promised scientific testing and validation of Dianetics, alienated many of the professionals who were involved in the early Dianetics movement.

As the members of the original Foundation in New Jersey began to defect, including John Campbell, the editor of *Astounding Science Fiction* and Hubbard's first supporter and benefactor, Hubbard's reaction was swift. He denounced each of them as Communists to the FBI, a dangerous action given the climate of McCarthyism at the time.

In spring, 1951, the Hubbard Dianetic Research Foundation in New Jersey was sued by the New Jersey Medical Association for teaching medicine without a license. With the resignations of Campbell and most of the other charter members of the Foundation, the New Jersey Foundation soon declared bankruptcy.

Hubbard produced a second book, *Science of Survival,* but it sold only 1,250 copies in its first printing. After his meteoric rise the previous year, he faced personal and public ruin, having squandered his fortune from the early success of Dianetics and having no prospects in sight.

Salvation came in the form of a knight in shining armor from Wichita, Kansas. Don Purcell, a self-made millionaire who was an early convert to Dianetics, invited Hubbard to Wichita with the promise of salvaging his beleaguered Dianetics empire.

The Hubbard Dianetics Research Foundation was reborn in Wichita, Kansas. Success remained elusive, however, as only a trickle of students came to Wichita to sign up for Dianetics training and Hubbard's lectures.

The honeymoon between Hubbard and Purcell was short-lived. Hubbard spent money faster than Purcell could provide it. He hadn't anticipated the hundreds of thousands of dollars in debts he legally acquired from the now-defunct earlier foundations, and, as a conservative man, Purcell was disturbed by Hubbard's blossoming interest in past lives.

In February, 1952, the Wichita Foundation was forced to file for bankruptcy. A nasty battle ensued between Hubbard and Purcell. Hubbard sued Purcell for reneging on his contract to assume the debts of the earlier foundations. Purcell, realizing that Hubbard had taken the mailing lists and other property of the Wichita Foundation, obtained a restraining order requiring Hubbard to return foundation property. The feud between the two men continued for months.

Hubbard opened the Hubbard College on the other side of Wichita. It remained open for only six weeks, but that was long enough for him to organize a convention, which, though scantily attended, provided him with a forum from which to announce a completely new development.

It was called Scientology, from the Latin *scio,* knowledge, and the Greek *logos,* to study. Scientology, the study of knowledge, would replace the study and practice of Dianetics, especially since Don Purcell owned all the Dianetics copyrights. As Dianetics concerned the body, Hubbard explained, Scientology addressed the soul, or the "thetan" in Scientology. Through Scientology, he claimed, a person could attain previously unreachable levels of spiritual awareness.

Shortly after making that announcement to a small group of devotees in Wichita, Hubbard, having secured divorces from his two previous wives, married for the third and final time to Mary Sue Whipp, a young student who had come from Texas to study at the Wichita Foundation.

Hubbard and Mary Sue packed their bags and headed to Phoenix. There, like the city's namesake, the fledgling science of Scientology arose from the ashes of Dianetics and soared to success.

The Hubbard Association of Scientology in Phoenix became the new world headquarters for Hubbard and Scientology. In his lectures and writing, he expounded the principles of this new "science," introducing a new cosmology and new direction for auditing.

The thetan, according to Hubbard, had been around for a long time. In the beginning, thetans together created the universe. However, over the eons, they devolved into a degraded state, becoming the effect of the universe they created. In his current debilitated state as a thetan, man is unaware of his actual identity as an immortal being.

The process of deterioration was expedited by a process called "implanting," in which thetans were subjected to high-voltage laser beams to program them for various purposes. Those implants were carried out within various locations in the universe and our own solar system. According to Hubbard, each of us, when we die, is subconsciously programmed to return to the nearest implant station in space, where our memories of the life we lived will be electronically zapped away, and we'll be programmed for our next life. Then we're sent back to earth to "pick up a new body" in an endless cycle of rebirth that has lasted for trillions of years.

Through Scientology auditing, the electronic "charge" resulting from the implants can be removed, supposedly restoring the person to levels of ability not achieved "in this sector of the universe," for millions of years. As the electronic charge is removed, the restored thetan, called an "operating thetan," or OT, will theoretically regain many lost abilities from his "native state," such as extrasensory perception, telepathy, telekinesis, and full control of his present body.

As an OT, a person through Scientology auditing should regain the ability to "exteriorize" at will from his body, becoming able to travel to any location in the universe and to control the body at a distance.

Simultaneously, Hubbard also introduced a curious gadget he called the "E-meter," short for electropsychometer. That small box-like instrument is actually a galvanic skin response monitor that registers changes in skin conductivity caused, according to Scientology, by emotional upset. The face of the E-meter contains a dial on which a needle registers "rises" and "falls" of emotional "charge." Various knobs alter the sensitivity of the needle reaction. Connected to the box are two leads running from two small soup or juice cans, which the preclear holds in his hands.

The E-meter helps the auditor probe the preclear's subconscious mind, looking for areas of emotional charge to be explored in auditing.

Scientologists believe that auditing, with the help of the E-meter, entirely confirms the existence of past lives. They believe that through Scientology auditing, immortality can be achieved by modern man. Those were the promises Hubbard made in his new science.

During that time, Hubbard introduced a policy of tithing, in which ten percent of each Scientology organization's weekly gross income was paid directly to Hubbard. Although he told Scientologists in a bulletin entitled *What Your Fees Buy* that he made no money from Scientology, that was a blatant lie. During the organization's later years, as much as one million dollars per week was channeled directly into Hubbard's personal accounts.

Hubbard wrote another book during that time called *What to Audit,* later renamed *The History of Man,* which one author judged correctly as "possibly the most absurd book ever written."[7]

In that book, Hubbard traced the history of the thetan, which he claimed came to earth only 35,000 years earlier. The book begins:

> This is a cold-blooded and
> factual account of your last sixty
> trillion years.

It also states that through the book's knowledge:

> the blind again see, the
> lame walk, the ill recover, the
> insane become sane, and the
> sane become saner.

---

[7] Ibid, p. 204

During those sixty trillion years, we passed through stages called the Jack in the Box, the Halver, Facsimile One, the Joiner, the Ice Cube, the Emanator, and the Between lives implants. All those implants could, of course, be nullified through Scientology auditing.

According to Hubbard's son, the book was written while Hubbard was on drugs. That's the only explanation that makes sense.

In the fall of 1952, Hubbard and his wife journeyed to London, England, where, one month later, Hubbard's first child by his third wife was born, a daughter named Diana. Hubbard wanted to oversee the new organization of Scientology in London and bring it firmly under his control.

When he returned to the States, Hubbard stopped in Philadelphia to give a series of lectures, packaged and still sold in Scientology as the *Philadelphia Doctorate Course*. Hubbard was, by then, offering both a bachelor's and a doctor's degree in Scientology.

Desiring a degree himself, Hubbard arranged with Sequoia University, a diploma mill in California that was shut down by the California Department of Education in 1958, to receive an honorary PhD, and he proudly displayed that credential after his name for some time. Years later, when it became public that the degree was phony, Hubbard issued an official policy renouncing the degree.

In 1952, Hubbard published another new book, *Scientology 8-8008*. The first eight in the title symbolized infinity. The next two digits, 80, symbolized the power of the physical universe reduced to zero. The final 08 symbolized the power of the personal universe of the person taken from zero to infinity. In other words, he said that through Scientology techniques, a person could eventually become a god.

Examples of some of the miraculous procedures include the following commands:

> Be three feet back of your head.
>
> Whatever you're looking at, copy it one at a time, many, many times. Then locate a nothingness and copy it many, many times.
>
> Locate the two upper-back corners of the room, hold on to them, and don't think.
>
> Now find a place where you are not.
>
> What would it be all right for you to look at here in this room?
>
> Now find something it's safe to look at outside this room.
>
>> Be near the Earth.
>> Be near the Moon.
>> Be near the Sun.
>> Be near the Earth.
>> Be near Mars.
>> Be at the center of Mars.

During the lectures in Philadelphia, Hubbard first mentioned the name of Aleister Crowley, an infamous Satanist in England during the first half of the century, whom he called, "my very good friend."

Crowley was, in fact, Hubbard's mentor, and remained so throughout his life. From Crowley's work, Hubbard found the inspiration for much of the bizarre material on the secret "upper levels" or "OT levels" of Scientology.

One day while Hubbard was lecturing in Philadelphia, US marshals arrived and arrested him for the theft of $9,000 from the Wichita Foundation. Amazingly, that was the only time Hubbard was in jail, though he was relentlessly pursued by various government agencies for the rest of his life.

Perhaps that arrest warned him of future problems. At that time, he began to mention to friends that he might transform Scientology into a church for legal protection and tax purposes. He knew that as a church, his organization would be given protections it otherwise lacked.

Accordingly, in December, 1953, Hubbard incorporated the Church of Scientology and the Church of American Science. One year later, the Church of Scientology in California was incorporated as a subsidiary of the Church of American Science.

In its Articles of Incorporation, the Church of American Science sounded vaguely like a Christian church. Included in the purposes in the original charter were:

> To train and indoctrinate ministers and brothers and sisters in the principles and teachings of the Church of American Science.

> To prepare them and ordain them to carry forward the work of the Church of American Science, and to conduct churches and minister to and conduct congregations.

> To resolve the travail and difficulties of members of congregations, as they may appertain to the spirit.

> To conduct seminaries and

instruction groups.[8]

Listed in the church's Creed are:

> That God works within
> Man his wonders to perform.
>
> That Man is his own soul,
> basically free and immortal, but
> deluded by the flesh.
>
> That Man has a God-given
> right to his own life.
>
> That Man has a God-given
> right to his own beliefs.
>
> That a civilization is lost
> when God and the spirit are
> forgotten by its leaders and its
> people.[9]

In the beginning of 1954 came the birth of the first actual Scientology "church," the Church of Scientology of California, as well as the birth of Hubbard's second child by Mary Sue, a son named Quentin. A second church was soon formed in Auckland, New Zealand.

Hubbard registered the umbrella organization, the Hubbard Association of Scientology International, to oversee all of his new churches.

Once he had churches, he needed "ministers," so he created the Scientology minister's course, in which Scientologists learned to perform the "sacred ceremonies" of Scientology, including weddings, christenings, and funerals.

The christening ceremony goes as follows:

> "Here we go." (To the child:)
> "How are you? All right. Now

---

[8] Original Articles of Incorporation, Church of American Science

[9] Creed of the Church of American Science

your name is _____. You got
that? Good. There you are. Did
that upset you? Now, do you
realize that you're a member of
the HASI? Pretty good, huh?"

The child is introduced to
his parents and godparents. The
ceremony concludes with, "Now
you're suitably christened. Don't
worry about it. It could be worse.
OK. Thank you very much.
They'll treat you all right."[10]

In 1955, the "Founding Church of Scientology" in Washington, DC, became the new world headquarters of Scientology.

In 1956, in Washington, DC, Hubbard held an Anti-Radiation Congress, at which he revealed that Scientologists could become radiation proof by taking niacin tablets, which he sold under the name Dianazene. Shortly after the congress, the FDA arrived and seized 21,000 illegal tablets. That was the beginning of his trouble with the FDA.

By July, 1957, more than 100 Scientology organizations existed in the United States, and they were flourishing.

In 1958, Scientology's tax-exempt status was denied. The Washington, DC, church appealed to the US Court of Claims, which upheld the original decision, ruling that Hubbard and his wife were profiting beyond "reasonable remuneration" from Scientology. At that time, Hubbard received a ten-percent tithe from all organizations worldwide and also received a $108,000 gift from the church. Mary Sue also received money from the church.

---

[10] Miller, p. 228

Hubbard's paranoia was greatly exacerbated by those encounters with government agencies. He began issuing policies railing against the "enemies" of Scientology, stating that the only way to deal with them was to attack even harder.

> If attacked on some
> vulnerable point by anyone or
> anything or any organization,
> always find or manufacture
> enough threat against them to
> cause them to sue for peace....
> Don't ever defend, always attack.
> Don't ever do nothing.
> Unexpected attacks in the rear of
> the enemy's front ranks work
> best. [11]

Hubbard had been spending more and more time in Europe. In the spring of 1959, he surprised his American followers with the purchase of a large Georgian manor in East Grinstead, England, which would become the new international headquarters of Scientology.

To hide the fact that his new home, named St. Hill, was the seat of the worldwide management and control center for Scientology, Hubbard made it known locally that he was conducting important horticultural experiments in the greenhouse of his new estate. He claimed that by bombarding plants with radiation, he could greatly increase their yields. He also pioneered the auditing of tomatoes, by connecting plants to the E-meter and claiming they registered pain when he pinched off a leaf.

Those experiments attracted quite a bit of press, and a photograph of Hubbard looking balefully at one of his mutant tomatoes was published in *Newsweek*.

---

[11] Ibid, p. 241

In an effort to generate good public relations with the locals in East Grinstead, Hubbard ran unopposed for the position of Road Safety Organizer for the town. He initially attacked his duties with enthusiasm, delivering lectures on road safety to the natives. Soon, however, he resigned, claiming he was too busy.

In the spring of 1961, Hubbard created on paper the Department of Official Affairs, a precursor to the notorious Guardian's Office of Scientology, his private intelligence agency.

In March, 1961, Hubbard created the St. Hill Special Briefing Course, a comprehensive training course for auditors during which students had to listen to as many as 600 tape recorded lectures, each sixty-to-ninety-minutes long, of Hubbard droning on about some esoteric aspect of auditing.

Soon, throngs of students from the United States and other countries arrived at St. Hill for the highly regarded privilege of studying directly under Ron, who presided as "Lord of the Manor."

The Hubbard family, which had by then expanded to include two more children, lived in style at St. Hill. They had a personal staff of seven, including a butler for Ron and a nurse and tutor for the children. The butler served Hubbard his accustomed drink, Coca-Cola, on a silver tray.

At St. Hill, Hubbard instituted the practice in all Scientology organizations of "security checking"— interrogations carried out on the E-meter. Those "sec checks" probed for any and all incriminating information about the person's past and current lives. The dossier thus compiled on every person in Scientology was forwarded to St. Hill, where it was filed to be used in the future against anyone who tried to defect from the organization.

In 1962, Hubbard sent a letter to President Kennedy, magnanimously offering the services of the Scientology auditors to audit the astronauts in the space program. Hubbard claimed that auditing would greatly increase the men's reaction times and other abilities critical to their missions. He felt deflated when no reply came.

On January 4, 1963, the FDA carried out a surprise raid on the Scientology organization in Washington, DC, carrying off nearly three tons of equipment and literature. The FDA subsequently brought a Federal case against Scientology for illegally using the E-meter as a medical instrument. As a result of that case, Scientologists were forced to label their E-meters with a disclaimer stating they weren't to be used to diagnose or treat illness but were only for religious counseling.

Scientology's legal problems were just beginning. Later in 1963, the government of Victoria, Australia, initiated a Board of Inquiry into Scientology as a result of complaints by people claiming they'd been defrauded.

The Board of Inquiry was carried out by Kevin Anderson, a member of the Victorian Parliament. After a two-year investigation, he published his findings in a report that was rabidly critical of Scientology. The report stated:

> Scientology is evil; its
> techniques evil; its practice a
> serious threat to the community,
> medically, morally, and socially;
> and its adherents sadly deluded
> and often mentally ill. [12]

As for Hubbard, Anderson stated that his sanity was to be:

> gravely doubted. His
> writing, abounding in self-
> glorification and grandiosity,

---

[12] Ibid, p. 252

replete with histrionics and hysterical, incontinent outbursts, was the product of a person of unsound mind. His teachings about thetans and past lives were nonsensical; he had a persecution complex; he had a great fear of matters associated with women and a prurient and compulsive urge to write in the most disgusting and derogatory way on such subjects as abortions, intercourse, rape, sadism, perversion, and abandonment. His propensity for neologisms was commonplace in the schizophrenic, and his compulsion to invent increasingly bizarre theories was strongly indicative of paranoid schizophrenia with delusions of grandeur—symptoms common to dictators.[13]

Anderson concluded his report by stating:

Scientology is a delusional belief system, based on fiction and fallacies and propagated by falsehood and deception.... What it really is, however, is the world's largest organization of unqualified persons engaged in the practice of dangerous techniques which masquerade as mental therapy.[14]

---

[13] Ibid, p. 252

[14] Ibid, p. 253

As a result of the Anderson Report, the Victoria Parliament passed the Psychological Practices Act, banning the practice and teaching of Scientology in that province.

Scientologists responded by simply changing the name of the Victoria church to Church of the New Faith, in which they continued to teach and practice Scientology.

In 1966, possibly taking a cue from the Victoria Inquiry, Health Minister Kenneth Robinson of the English House of Commons was asked to begin an inquiry into Scientology.

Hubbard responded to those attacks by creating a new branch of the organization called the Public Investigation Section, staffed by private investigators who compiled dossiers on each of the "enemies" of Scientology. One of them was given the task of investigating and compiling a dossier on every psychiatrist in England.

The Public Investigation Section soon evolved into the Guardian's Office of Scientology, a private intelligence organization designed to "deal with any threats to Scientology." Mary Sue Hubbard was appointed the Comptroller for the GO.

Meanwhile, Hubbard had been spending his time refining the "tech" and the organizational structure of Scientology. A system of "ethics" was established as a form of social control within Scientology. Lower-level auditing was standardized into a series of hierarchical "grades" of auditing through which each preclear would progress on the road to Clear.

In 1966, the "world's first Clear" was announced for the second time, that time without a public demonstration of his powers. John McMaster, a benign and much loved disciple of Hubbard's, received this distinction, much to his own surprise. After becoming the world's first Clear, he served for a time as Hubbard's personal ambassador to Scientologists around the world, until he, too, eventually ran afoul of Hubbard's temper and was reduced to Scientology's lowest rank. He later left Scientology and spoke scathingly of the man he served so faithfully.

In 1966, Hubbard went to Rhodesia, having "discovered" during auditing that in one of his past lives, he was Cecil Rhodes, the British financier and administrator of that country. For some time, he'd been looking for a more accommodating country in which to establish Scientology's world headquarters. Perhaps that was in his mind as he journeyed to Rhodesia.

Arriving in Rhodesia, he set out to conquer the hearts and minds of those in power, socializing with all the right people and speaking on public TV to ingratiate himself with the natives. In the end, however, he completely alienated the Rhodesian officials with his opinionated views of Rhodesian politics and was soon expelled from the country.

If Hubbard's ego was temporarily deflated by that enforced exile, it was restored when he returned to England and was welcomed by hundreds of jubilant, cheering Scientologists at the airport.

In 1966, Hubbard wrote a policy stating that he was resigning his position of President and Executive Director of Scientology, probably for legal reasons. However, evidence and witnesses to the contrary prove that he remained in direct control of the church and its bank accounts for many years to come.

Back in England, Hubbard soon felt more pressure. Scientology became a subject for debate in the British Parliament. There was a recent scandal in East Grinstead in which a young girl, a Scientologist with a prior history of schizophrenia, was discovered by police wandering the streets in the middle of the night in an incoherent condition.

Police began interrogating Scientologists as they arrived at St. Hill. Eventually, the British used the Aliens Act to keep Scientologists out of the country, but that was easily circumvented by Scientologists listing other reasons to visit.

Despite all the problems, business at St. Hill was booming. In spite of, or perhaps because of, the adverse publicity received during that time, income increased exponentially. Meanwhile, Hubbard, sensing the increasingly hostile climate in England, conceived a daring plan.

Toward the end of 1966, the Hubbard Exploration Company, Limited, was registered in London. Simultaneously, a select group of core Scientologists arrived at St. Hill to begin training on a secret project called the "Sea Project." Hubbard quietly purchased two ships, a small schooner named the *Enchanter,* and a larger, 414-ton trawler named the *Avon River.* Crews of Scientologists were assigned to those ships and spent many long, hard hours scrubbing and refitting them, as well as completing basic training in seamanship.

Hubbard said good-bye to St. Hill and flew to North Africa, where he planned to rendezvous with the ships. While waiting for them to arrive, he bought a third ship, a 3,280-ton cattle ferry called the *Royal Scotsman.* The ship was hurriedly registered in Sierra Leone to bypass British regulations that prevented it from sailing.

By then, the Sea Project, soon renamed the "Sea Organization" or "Sea Org," as it's known today, began to take form. Members wore naval-looking uniforms and drilled in the basic points of seamanship in anticipation of going to sea.

It was a daring plan. To escape the regulation of troublesome bureaucracies, as well as the investigations and inquiries of unfriendly governments, Hubbard withdrew to the one place where he could govern Scientology without outside interference—the sea.

Miraculously, after a few frightening near disasters during the first trial runs at sea, the novice Scientology crews survived the vagaries of the Mediterranean and successfully piloted even the unwieldy *Royal Scotsman* from one Mediterranean port to another.

Hubbard sent for his family from St. Hill and moved aboard the *Royal Scotsman* with them, which became known as the Flagship or "Flag" of the fleet. He began to release secret, "upper levels" of Scientology, known as OT levels, and students soon began arriving at the ship to train on those levels. Much of the ship was converted to classrooms and auditing rooms to accommodate the students. They considered it a great honor and opportunity to train so close to "Source," Ron Hubbard.

Hubbard's disposition aboard ship, as always, was mercurial. According to those who were there, he was sometimes jovial and charming, loving to sit and regale his followers with tales of his exploits on other planets and in other galaxies, while at other times, he became a bellowing monster, exploding in rage at the "incompetent and stupid" people around him who were plotting to "destroy him."

In one of his bursts of temper, he originated the bizarre practice of "overboarding," which served as punishment for those unlucky enough to have crossed him in some way on the ship. Early each morning, the students were ordered to line up on the deck while a list was read of all those who had failed in some way during the previous day, either through technical errors during their auditing or in the performance of shipboard duties.

When the names were read, each person called would be thrown overboard into the cold water that was anywhere from fifteen to forty feet below. It was an understandably traumatic experience for the unfortunates to whom that punishment was administered, particularly as no one was exempt through virtue of age or lack of the ability to swim. That punishment was part of the elaborate system of "ethics" established earlier by Hubbard throughout Scientology.

Another form of "ethics" that was common onboard the ship was the imprisonment of offending Sea Org members and even children in the filthy, dangerous chain lockers in the bowels of the ship. In one case, a four-year-old boy was cast into the locker as punishment for eating some telex tape.

Ethics punishments were also carried out in the Scientology organizations on land in similarly degrading, cruel ways. Dunking in freezing water, having one's head dunked in a toilet while it was being flushed, and being locked in closets for extended periods of time often substituted for the shipboard practice of overboarding.

The security and anonymity that Hubbard hoped to achieve at sea eluded him, however, as the strange goings-on aboard ship succeeded in antagonizing officials in local ports. The daily practice of overboarding, carried out in full view of locals on shore, accompanied by the fact that a large percentage of the ships' crews were female, fueled a dangerous rumor circulating throughout the area that the Scientology ships were, in fact, CIA ships.

While docked at the port of Corfu, Greece, Hubbard felt he had finally found a stable port for his ships. He proceeded as usual, trying to ingratiate himself with the local authorities by expansive promises to bring prosperity to the area by building hotels, roads, factories, golf courses, and even a university of philosophy on the island. He orchestrated a lavish and public "renaming ceremony" to which the local authorities were invited and in which the ships were renamed the *Diana,* the *Athena,* and the *Apollo* as part of a demonstration of Hubbard's affinity for all things Greek.

Unfortunately, the British consul on the island, having been tipped off by his own government concerning the true nature of the "mystery ships," and perhaps fearing a Scientology takeover of the local government, informed the authorities. Hubbard and his ships were given twenty-four hours to depart Greece.

On land, Scientology organizations were also encountering trouble. In England, the Scientology Prohibition Act was passed, barring foreigners from entering the country to study or practice Scientology. In Rhodesia, a ban on importing Scientology material was passed. In Perth, Australia, the local Scientology organization was raided by the police. New inquiries were undertaken in New Zealand and South Africa.

The popular John McMaster resigned from Scientology, and in the US, it was revealed that Charles Manson had studied and practiced Scientology before inciting his followers to commit their savage murders in Los Angeles. Also in the US, the IRS began investigating Scientology.

The Sea Org, meanwhile, hastily relocated to the port of Tangier, Morocco, and the Scientologists once again embarked on a campaign to win over the locals. Hubbard had renewed hopes for finding a homeport for Scientology. Scientologists offered their services to the army and the secret police, demonstrating the E-meter and its applicability in ferreting out traitors and secret agents.

However, the faction of the government to which they made their overtures carried out an unsuccessful coup attempt, and all were executed. Scientologists were lucky to escape without incident.

Word reached Hubbard that Scientology was about to be indicted in France, and that French officials were going to seek Hubbard's extradition for prosecution in their fraud case against the church. Hubbard flew to New York, where he hid in a small apartment in Queens for nine months with a few of his loyal Sea Org members until the crisis passed.

Nine months later, although he was indicted in absentia in France for fraud, it was deemed safe for him to return to the ship. Shortly afterward, Hubbard suffered a motorcycle accident on Tenerife in the Canary Islands in which he broke an arm and several ribs. Never a good patient, during the weeks of his convalescence Hubbard was in an unusually foul mood, even for him. During one of his black moods, he conceived of a new punishment as part of the Scientology ethics system—the Rehabilitation Project Force, or RPF.

The RPF was, in effect, a prison, and it was quickly put into practice at most of the major Scientology organizations worldwide. It has since become the dread of every Scientology staff member.

As a disciplinary measure within Scientology, any staff member falling into disfavor for any reason could be assigned to the RPF. Conditions in the RPF are severe. The offending staff members can't bathe, must wear distinctive uniforms or a gray rag tied around the arm, can't speak unless spoken to, and are shunned by the rest of the group. They receive minimal sleep, live in inhumane conditions, and are sometimes fed leftover food from the plates of regular staff members.

On the ship, anyone who crossed Hubbard was subject to immediate demotion to the RPF. At one point, he established what was called the RPF's RPF for those unfortunate inhabitants of the regular RPF who were insufficiently broken in will and needed further "rehabilitation."

As Hubbard grew increasingly paranoid, he collected around himself a group of youngsters, mostly female, who were children of veteran Sea Org members. That group was named the Commodore's Messenger Organization, or CMO. They were trained to deliver messages on the ship. When given an order by Hubbard, they were trained to run to the recipient of the order and deliver it in the exact tone of voice and volume that Hubbard used. They soon developed into a powerful, feared group onboard the ship.

In many ways, those young Scientologists perfectly suited Hubbard's needs. Many knew little of life outside Scientology. They were impressionable and malleable and were trained to become young clones of Hubbard, fanatic and ruthless. They were unquestioningly devoted to him and competed among themselves to find new ways to please him.

They also served as his personal attendants, waking him in the morning, laying out his clothes, helping him dress, smearing his face with creams, waiting on him, following him about the ship, and carrying ashtrays to catch falling ash from his cigarettes. No leader ever had a more devoted retinue of servants than Hubbard with his CMO. It was a two-way street. As Hubbard became increasingly paranoid through his later years, he grew to trust no one except the children of the CMO, who would eventually inherit the church.

Rumors circulated throughout the Mediterranean that the Scientology ships were running drugs, working for the CIA, or engaged in white-slave traffic. As a result, it became increasingly dangerous for the ships to dock. Those tensions peaked in the Portuguese port of Funchal on the island of Madeira when an angry mob pelted the *Apollo* with rocks and bottles, injuring several Scientologists during the melee.

Hubbard ordered the ship to sail due west. The staff realized they were heading back to America, which many hadn't seen for years. The *Apollo* was one hour from Charleston, South Carolina when a frantic radio signal from shore warned of impending danger.

A welcoming party comprised of Immigration officials, the DEA, US Customs, the FBI, the Coast Guard, and several US Marshals was waiting for them, ready to arrest Hubbard. So Hubbard ordered the ship to sail to the Bahamas. For a year, the ship sailed an elusive course throughout the Caribbean, staying at one island port after another.

In 1975, while docked in Curacao in the Netherlands Antilles, Hubbard suffered a heart attack and had to be taken to the local hospital. He spent several weeks in the Curacao Hilton, being nursed to health by his faithful disciples.

Soon, however, as it had in the Mediterranean, the ship with its strange crew began arousing suspicion in Caribbean ports, and Hubbard knew that his quest for safety at sea was over. He sent scouts ahead to find property for sale on the Florida coast.

They reported there was a large hotel for sale in Clearwater, Florida, which was quickly purchased for $2.3 million in cash under the phony name of the United Churches of Florida. The Sea Org moved into its new headquarters, and Hubbard was settled in a suite of apartments in a nearby town.

Soon the Clearwater natives, curious about the army of secretive, uniformed young people inhabiting the "religious retreat" in the old Fort Harrison Hotel, began to investigate. A resourceful newspaper reporter was the first one to make the connection to Scientology. As the church continued to purchase more and more property in the small tourist town, tension rose between the citizens and the Scientologists. Despite efforts by the Scientologists to conquer the hearts of the Clearwater natives with a succession of carefully orchestrated public-relations campaigns, those tensions still exist today.

On another front, Hubbard had long been preoccupied with the problem of discovering what information existed about his organization in the files of government agencies. Because it would take a relatively long time to gain access to those files under the Freedom of Information Act, he conceived a plan to gain the information in a more direct way.

He called the plan "Operation Snow White," not because of the fairytale character of that name, but because he considered that once the government files were "cleaned" of the damaging information about Scientology, they'd look snow white.

Within the Guardian's Office of Scientology, the branch of the organization that routinely trained "operatives" and "agents" to carry out various covert church operations, plans were laid to infiltrate a select list of government agencies.

In the mid-70's, a GO staff member named Gerald Wolfe secured a job as a typist for the IRS. Using his official ID badge, he and another GO member named Michael Meisner carried out several successful burglaries in a dozen different IRS and Department of Justice offices, managing to illicitly photocopy and steal tens of thousands of government documents.

The break-ins continued with impunity for more than eighteen months. In June, 1976, a suspicious guard alerted the FBI, and the two men were stopped during one of their missions and questioned about their activities. Shortly afterward, Gerald Wolfe was arrested, and a warrant was issued for the arrest of Michael Meisner.

Although the Guardian's Office quickly put into effect an elaborate plan to protect Scientology from being implicated in the burglaries, their efforts were sabotaged when Meisner, who was being kept prisoner by the church, escaped and turned state's evidence for the FBI.

On July 7, 1977, 134 FBI agents carried out surprise raids on the headquarters of Scientology in Washington, DC, and Los Angeles. They seized over 48,000 documents and subsequently indicted eleven top GO agents, including Mary Sue Hubbard, who, as Comptroller of the GO, was ultimately responsible for its criminal activities.

Hubbard, learning of the raids, immediately fled into hiding in Nevada, leaving his wife to take the blame for the crimes he originated.

On October 26, 1979, US District Judge Charles Richey sentenced nine of the eleven GO officials to prison, including Hubbard's wife, who served one year of a five-year sentence before being paroled. After the arrests, Hubbard distanced himself from his wife, seeing her for the last time in 1979.

Hubbard directed the Sea Org to purchase several properties in remote locations in southern California, where he would spend the rest of his days hiding from the world and the "enemies" he believed to be constantly pursuing him.

He took a cadre of young people from the CMO with him into the desert near Palm Springs. At one point, he assembled a movie studio on one of his desert properties and endeavored to produce movies for the enlightenment of the general population. Most of the movies were lurid documentaries about the savagery of psychiatrists and other "enemies."

Hubbard had been plagued by poor health for many years. In September, 1978, he suffered a severe pulmonary embolism and nearly died, yet he lived for another eight years.

When his whereabouts were compromised by a defecting Sea Org member, Hubbard was forced to flee once more to an even more remote location. For the last five years of his life, he remained in hiding on a large ranch in Creston, California, where he lived quietly with three of his most loyal CMO aides.

In a massive reorganization within the church in the early 1980s, and with the silent support of Hubbard, the children of the CMO, now grown into young adults, began to exert their authority over the rest of the Scientology organization. The "old guard" upper-echelon executives within Scientology were removed from power during an internal purge.

The network of independent "missions," lower-level Scientology organizations offering introductory services and supplying the more advanced organizations with customers, were taken over, or nationalized, by the CMO. The mission holders were forced to turn over all their assets to the "new guard" or risk being expelled from the organization.

In 1976, Quentin, Hubbard's oldest son, committed suicide. His oldest daughter defected from the cult. His two youngest children are still reportedly in the organization. His wife has been in seclusion since her release from prison in 1980.

On January 19, 1986, Hubbard issued his last communication to his organization, in which he promoted himself from commodore to admiral.

On January 24, 1986, Hubbard died at his remote ranch in Creston, California, of a cerebral hemorrhage. Although an autopsy wasn't performed, his fingerprints matched those on file with the FBI and the Department of Justice.

Three days later, it was announced to the assembled Scientologists in Los Angeles that L. Ron Hubbard had:

> moved on to his next level
> of research, a level beyond the
> imagination and in a state
> exterior to the body. The body he
> had used to facilitate his
> existence in this universe had
> ceased to be useful and in fact
> had become an impediment to
> the work he now must do outside
> its confines.

His followers were told, and fully believe that:

> L. Ron Hubbard used this
> lifetime and body we knew to
> accomplish what no man has
> ever accomplished—he unlocked
> the mysteries of life and gave
> Scientologists the tools to free
> themselves and their fellow
> man.... [15]

Today, some 40,000 dedicated Scientologists in the US and a total of 100,000 worldwide carry on the "vital" work of Scientology, which they believe will free mankind.

---

[15] Ibid, p. 375

CHAPTER TWO

L. Ron Hubbard—Messiah or Madman?

It is worthy of note that the most notorious quacks, often men of genius and education, though mentally ill-balanced, and morally of low standards, have been great travelers and shrewd observers of human nature. When such a one becomes ambitious to acquire wealth, he is likely to prove a dangerous person in the community.

Robert Means Lawrence, 1910

Ironically...most messiahs have had markedly unstable lives. Their backgrounds and life histories are rife with traumatic experiences. It is commonplace among them that their calling is precipitated by crisis, nervous breakdown, and physical collapse. Most messiahs are people who have been unable to successfully integrate themselves into ordinary society. They are marginal individuals—members of groups denied access to power,

> or individuals who for a variety of
> reasons have failed to achieve it.
> As a group, messiahs also
> display other characteristics.
> They are ambitious, intelligent,
> and rigid; thus, despite their
> inability to follow the usual
> routes to success, they manage
> to create their own.
>
> Willa Appel, *Cults in America*

To his followers, L. Ron Hubbard was larger than life. The biographies of Hubbard given within the cult portray the metamorphosis of this legendary man in stages from youthful prodigy, to teenager adventurer, to brave war hero, to the long-suffering messiah who gave his life for all. It would seem only logical that a man of the extraordinary accomplishments boasted of by Hubbard would have had an equally extraordinary life.

Unfortunately, while the legendary accomplishments of this cult guru might have made interesting fodder for one of his swashbuckling adventure novels, the true facts of his life reveal quite another picture. As with the Wizard of Oz, once the curtain was drawn, the fearsome wizard was just an ordinary man. So it was with Hubbard. His "official biography" states:

> L. Ron Hubbard was born
> in Tilden, Nebraska, on the 13th
> of March, 1911. His father was
> Commander Harry Ross Hubbard
> of the United States Navy. His
> mother was Dora May
> Hubbard....[16]

---

[16] Corydon, p. 219

So far, everything is true. Because his father was away at sea, his biographer continues:

> Ron spent his early
> childhood years on his
> grandfather's large cattle ranch
> in Montana, said to cover a
> quarter of the state. It was on
> this ranch that he learned to
> read and write by the time he
> was three-and-a-half years old.[17]

The truth is that Hubbard's grandfather was a small-town veterinarian who didn't own a cattle ranch in Montana. After Hubbard and his parents relocated to Helena, Montana, where his father was hired to manage a local theater, the grandparents soon followed, bought a house on Fifth Avenue, and the grandfather opened the Capital City Coal Company.

In another biography, Hubbard boasted that his great-grandfather, I. C. De Wolfe, was a distinguished sea captain. It's not known whether the great-grandfather was a sea captain. However, the initials IC belonged to his great-grandmother, not great-grandfather.

The story continues:

> L. Ron Hubbard found the
> life of a young rancher very
> enjoyable. Long days were spent
> riding, breaking broncos, hunting
> coyote, and taking his first steps
> as an explorer. For it was in
> Montana that he had his first
> encounter with the Blackfoot
> Indians. He became a blood
> brother of the Blackfoot... When
> he was ten years old, he rejoined

---

[17] Ibid, p. 219

his family...[18]

Although those events may've existed in the imagination of a young boy in Montana, that is the only place where they did, in fact, exist.

Young Ron Hubbard lived with his parents in a small apartment on Rodney Street in Helena, and he attended the local kindergarten. His grandparents and his lively maternal aunts lived nearby. When he was six-years old, his father enlisted in the Navy after the start of World War I. For the next few years, Ron and his mother followed Harry to a series of port cities where he was stationed.

> By the time he was twelve years old, young Ron Hubbard had read a large number of the world's greatest classics—and his interest in philosophy and religion was born. Ron Hubbard had the distinction of being the only boy in the country to secure an Eagle Scout badge at the age of twelve years. In Washington, DC, he had also become a close friend of President Coolidge's son, Calvin, Jr., whose early death accelerated L. Ron Hubbard's interest in the mind and spirit of man.[19]

Although Hubbard did receive an Eagle Scout badge at the age of thirteen, the Boy Scouts of America keeps only an alphabetical listing of Eagle Scouts with no record of their ages. During his thirteenth year, Hubbard was chosen to go with forty other scouts to shake President Coolidge's hand, who was being given an honor by the

---

[18] Ibid, p. 219

[19] Ibid, p. 220

Scouts. It's not known whether he became friends with the president's son.

The following years, from 1925 to 1929, saw the young Mr. Hubbard between the ages of fourteen and eighteen, as a budding and enthusiastic world traveler and adventurer. His father was sent to the Far East, and, having the financial support of his wealthy grandfather, L. Ron Hubbard spent these years journeying through Asia.[20]

He was up and down the China coast several times in his teens, from Ching Wong Tow to Hong Kong and inland to Peking and Manchuria.

In China, he met an old magician whose ancestors had served in the court of the Kublai Khan and a Hindu who could hypnotize cats. In the high hills of Tibet, he lived with bandits who accepted him because of his honest interest in them and their way of life.

In the remote reaches of western Manchuria, he made friends with the ruling warlords by demonstrating his horsemanship. On an island in the South Pacific, the fearless boy calmed the natives by exploring a cave that was

---

[20] Ibid, p. 220

> supposed to be haunted and
> showing them that the rumbling
> sound from within was nothing
> more sinister than an
> underground river. Deep in the
> jungles of Polynesia, he
> discovered an ancient burial
> ground steeped in the tradition of
> heroic warriors and kings...[21]

Heady adventures for a teenager!

The truth, however, is a bit more believable. At the age of thirteen, the Hubbards moved to Bremerton, Washington, where young Ron was an eighth grader at Union High School. He enjoyed activities such as hiking and camping at the nearby Boy Scout campground.

Two years later, when Ron was a sophomore at Queen Anne High School, his father was unexpectedly posted to Guam. It was decided that while his mother would join her husband in Guam for his two-year posting, Ron would live with his grandparents and aunts in Helena and finish high school.

However, to mollify Ron, the father suggested he spend part of the summer with them in Guam before returning to school. In May, 1927, Ron and his mother sailed to Guam on the steamship *President Madison,* with stops in Honolulu, Yokohama, Shanghai, Hong Kong, and Manila. Mother and son arrived in Guam in June, and Ron spent the month teaching English to native children who were apparently spellbound by his thatch of red hair.

In July, the young Hubbard sailed back home and was registered by September as a junior at Helena High School, where he joined the editorial staff of the school newspaper as the jokes editor.

---

[21] Miller, p. 26

In the spring of his junior year, however, Hubbard suddenly disappeared from home and school. There was a rumor that he fought with a teacher and didn't want to face expulsion. He went first to visit an aunt and uncle in nearby Seattle, then he caught a train for San Diego to catch a ship bound for Guam. He couldn't sail without his father's permission, but his father obligingly cabled the needed permission, and young Ron was bound for Guam again.

In Guam, his mother tutored him in preparation for college. In October, 1928, Ron accompanied his parents on a ten-day vacation to China, but he was unimpressed by the Chinese and wrote in his journal:

> They smell of all the baths
> they didn't take. The trouble with
> China is, there are too many
> chinks here.[22]

In his journals, Ron was already writing adventure stories, interspersing his more mundane studies in history and geometry with adventure stories in exotic, Oriental settings.

To his father's disappointment, Ron failed the entrance exam for the Annapolis Naval Academy. Determined to get his son into the Academy, Harry enrolled Ron at the Swavely Preparatory School in Manassas, Virginia, in a special program for prospective Annapolis candidates. Inevitably, however, Ron was denied admission because of bad eyesight.

Next, Ron was enrolled in the Woodward School for Boys in Washington, DC, as a substitute for taking the College Entrance Examination. In September, 1930, Ron was admitted to George Washington University School of Engineering with a major in civil engineering.

---

[22] Ibid, p. 43

If ever there was a match that wasn't to be, it was between young Hubbard and the School of Engineering. Bored by studies in calculus, chemistry, and German, Ron immersed himself in starting a gliding club on the GWU campus. Ignoring his studies, he spent every possible minute at the nearby airfield and was soon licensed as a Commercial Glider Pilot.

Predictably, and to his parents' distress, Ron's grades for the first semester ranged from an A in physical education to a C in mechanical engineering, a D in chemistry, and F's in German and calculus, earning him a D average and placing him on scholastic probation.

Undaunted, Ron continued writing his stories. In January, 1932, his first professional article was published in *Sportsman Pilot,* a flying magazine.

During the summer of 1932, Ron organized the Caribbean Motion Picture Expedition, renting a four-masted schooner and planning a voyage with fifty other students to sixteen Caribbean ports of call, at which they'd make adventure movies.

However, the trip didn't turn out as planned. A storm at sea drove the ship off course, and they ended up in Bermuda, not Martinique. After leaving Bermuda, the fresh water leaked from the tanks, morale was at an ebb, and, when they finally reached Martinique, most of the disgruntled crew abandoned the ship for home. The ship's owners, realizing their fee was at risk, ordered the ship back to Baltimore where the trip began.

Although Ron was later to claim the trip was a great success, citing among its scientific accomplishments that rare specimens of flora and fauna were gathered for the University of Michigan, that underwater films were taken for the US Hydrographic Office, and that photographs of the trip were purchased by the New York *Times,* subsequent investigation proved none of those were true.

Ron returned to Washington, DC, to receive his grades for the previous semester. He earned a B in English, D's in calculus and electrical and magnetic physics, and F's in molecular and atomic physics. Realizing he was fighting a losing battle, he informed his parents he wouldn't return to college.

His father's solution to his son's educational failure was to send him on a trip to Puerto Rico, where the Red Cross needed volunteers. Ron used the trip to search for gold in the Puerto Rican countryside, working briefly as a field representative for a company called West Indies Minerals.

Despite his failure at school, Hubbard later frequently boasted that he'd been a student in the first course in atomic physics in the country and received an honorary PhD—which he renounced much later, when it was discovered and made public that the bogus degree had been purchased from a diploma mill in California.

The official biography of Hubbard continues:

> His first action on leaving college was to blow off steam by leading an expedition into Central America. In the next few years he headed three, all of them undertaken to study savage peoples and cultures and to provide fodder for his articles and stories. Between 1933 and 1941 he visited many barbaric cultures and yet found time to write seven million words of published fact and fiction.[23]

Although there is no evidence that Hubbard made any trips to Central America, there is evidence that when

---

[23] Ibid, p. 59

he arrived back in Washington, DC, from Puerto Rico, he married Mary Louise Grubb, nicknamed "Polly," and began his career as a struggling writer. In 1933, he sold four articles, receiving less than $100 for all, the rate of pay for pulp fiction writers at the time being a penny a word.

In 1934, his first child was born, a son named L. Ron, Jr., and, to keep pace with the rising expenses of a young family man, Hubbard began to produce fiction at a prolific rate, often writing a story a day. His writing habits were unique. He frequently wrote all night, retiring at dawn and sleeping until early afternoon.

Soon, his labor began paying off, as more and more of his stories were published, and Hubbard began to acquire a reputation among adventure writers. In 1935, his output included ten pulp novels, three novelettes, twelve short stories, and three nonfiction articles. The titles of his stories included *The Phantom Patrol, Destiny's Drum, Man-Killers of the Air, Hostage to Death,* and *Hell's Legionnaires.*[24]

Another child arrived in 1936, a daughter, Catherine. Hubbard moved his small family to Bremerton, Washington, where his parents settled, and where Ron and Polly bought a small house. He spent the next few years shuttling between Bremerton and New York City, where he made frequent trips to fraternize with fellow adventure writers. In gatherings with other writers, Hubbard was invariably the center of attention, entertaining the others with his yarns and tall tales.

In 1938, John Campbell, the editor of *Astounding Science Fiction* magazine, persuaded Ron to try his hand at science fiction. The result was successful, and Hubbard's stories in that genre began appearing regularly, alongside his usual adventure stories and westerns.

---

[24] Ibid, p. 68

During that same year, there was a curious story about Hubbard. He apparently began telling friends that he had an important book, *Excalibur,* which he claimed would have a greater impact on people than the Bible. He seemed quite excited about that book. He told his wife it would earn him a place in history, yet strangely, no one ever saw the book.

Hubbard claimed that the first six people who read the book were so overwhelmed by its contents, they went out of their minds. He claimed that the inspiration for the book came from an out-of-the-body experience he had under nitrous oxide while at the dentist. To prevent any more casualties, he claimed he hid the book. Although he mentioned the book from time to time, its existence was never proven.

In 1939 and 1940, Hubbard continued writing, producing several famous stories, such as *Fear, Typewriter in the Sky,* and *Final Blackout.* His stories are still known and read by science-fiction fans throughout the country, to whom the name L. Ron Hubbard is associated with science fiction, not a controversial cult.

In 1941, as the US was drawn into the Second World War, Hubbard was determined to enlist in the Navy. When a friend of his who was a senator obligingly gave him some official stationery, Hubbard composed his own letter of recommendation.

This will introduce one of the most brilliant men I have ever known: Captain L. Ron Hubbard.

He writes under six names in a diversity of fields, from political economy to action fiction, and, if he would make at least one of his pen names public, he would have little difficulty entering anywhere. He has published many millions of words and some fourteen movies.

In exploration, he has honorably carried the flag of the Explorer's Club and has extended geographical and mineralogical knowledge. He is well known in many parts of the world and has considerable influence in the Caribbean and Alaska.

As a key figure in writing organizations, he has considerable political worth, and in the Northwest, he is a powerful influence.

I have known him for many years and have found him discreet, loyal, honest, and without peer in the art of getting things done swiftly.

If Captain Hubbard requests help, be assured that it will benefit others more than himself.

For courage and ability, I cannot too strongly recommend him.[25]

In July, 1941, L. Ron Hubbard entered the Navy as a lieutenant in the US Naval Reserve.

Hubbard's stories of his naval career serve as an example of his most outrageous fiction writing. The official (Scientology) account of his naval career reads:

Commissioned before the war in 1941, by the US Navy,

---

[25] Ibid, p. 93

Hubbard was ordered to the Philippines at the outbreak of war in the US and was flown home in the late spring of 1942 in the Secretary of the Navy's private plane as the first US returned casualty from the Far East.

He served in the South Pacific, and in 1942 was relieved by fifteen officers of rank and was rushed home to take part in the 1942 battle against German submarines as Commanding Officer of a corvette serving in the north Atlantic. In 1943 he was made Commodore of Corvette Squadrons, and in 1944 he worked with amphibious forces. After serving in all five theaters of World War II and receiving twenty-one medals and palms, in 1944 he was severely wounded and taken crippled and blinded to Oak Knoll Naval Hospital.[26]

Another "official" biography continues:

Crippled and blinded at the end of the war, he resumed his studies of philosophy and by his discoveries recovered so fully that he was reclassified in 1949 for full combat duty. It is a matter of medical record that he has twice been pronounced dead and that in 1950 he was given a perfect

---

[26] Ibid, p. 95

score on mental and physical
fitness reports.

The truth about Hubbard's war career, although quite different, is no less interesting.

His first job in the Navy was a desk job in public relations. His job was to write stories featuring the American serviceman for various national publications. However, that didn't fit with the image Hubbard had of himself as war hero, so he soon requested, and was awarded, a transfer to Navy Intelligence.

On December 7, 1941, the Japanese bombed Pearl Harbor, and war was officially declared.

On December 18, 1941, Hubbard was posted as an intelligence officer to the Philippines. In Brisbane, Australia, while waiting for a ship to Manila, he managed to so antagonize his superior officers that he was sent home, with an entry in his record stating that:

> This officer is not
> satisfactory for independent duty
> assignment. He is garrulous and
> tries to give impressions of his
> importance. He also seems to
> think he has unusual ability in
> most lines. These characteristics
> indicate that he will require close
> supervision for satisfactory
> performance of any intelligence
> duty.

The report added that Hubbard had become *the source of much trouble.*[27]

Hubbard was sent to San Francisco and given a posting in the Office of the Cable Sensor, another desk job. Two months later, bored with his new duties,

---

[27] Ibid, p. 98

Hubbard requested sea duty and was made the commanding officer of the USS YP-422, a converted Navy gunboat.

Hubbard went to Neponset, Massachusetts, where the gunboat was being refitted, but he was relieved of command before the boat sailed due to a difficulty he had with the commandant of the Navy yard. Again a report was filed in his service record, stating that he was *not temperamentally fitted for independent command.*[28]

Anticipating another desk job, Hubbard's spirits rose when he found he was being sent to the Submarine Chaser Training Center in Miami, Florida.

After completion of his duties in Miami, and a ten-day antisubmarine-warfare course in Key West, Florida, Hubbard was once again entrusted by the Navy with the command of a 280-ton sub chaser, the USS PC-815.

In May, 1943, Hubbard sailed his ship out of the Navy shipyard in Portland, Oregon. He was to sail from Portland to San Diego for the first shakedown cruise.

Just off the Oregon coast, Hubbard and his crew made a surprise discovery of two enemy submarines in coastal waters, right in the middle of a busy shipping lane. Six depth charges were fired. Joined by another sub chaser, seven more charges were fired.

Soon, a US Coast Guard ship came to replenish the depleted supply of depth charges on Hubbard's ship. The PC-815 continued attacking, delivering all twenty-seven depth charges, and the crew anxiously scanned the water for signs of a destroyed enemy sub.

The PC-815 was ordered to return to shore, where an investigation was called into the unusual battle and because of the proximity of enemy submarines to the Oregon coast. The conclusion the investigating body

---

[28] Ibid, p. 99

reached was that there were no enemy submarines in the area, but there were known magnetic deposits. It seemed that Hubbard and his crew just fought a two-day battle with a suboceanic magnetic deposit. Hubbard, as expected, took some good-natured ribbing from other officers for his "battle," but he wasn't relieved of his command.

In May, 1943, he sailed to San Diego without misadventure, but, while moored off the San Diego coast, his ship strayed into Mexican territorial waters, and he ordered a test firing of the ship's guns directly at the nearby Coronado Islands.

An official complaint was lodged by the Mexican government, and a board of investigation was held, as a result of which Hubbard was again relieved of his duties and transferred.

In a fitness report covering Hubbard's Navy career to that point, he was evaluated as *below average,* and the following notation was placed in his record:

> Consider this officer
> lacking in the essential qualities
> of judgment, leadership, and
> cooperation. He acts without
> forethought as to probable
> results. He is believed to have
> been sincere in his efforts to
> make his ship efficient and
> ready. Not considered qualified
> for command or promotion at
> this time. Recommend duty on a
> large vessel where he can be
> properly supervised.[29]

After that, Hubbard spent three months in the naval hospital in San Diego, complaining of a variety of ailments

---

[29] Ibid, p. 107

from an ulcer to malaria to back pain. In a letter to his family, he reported he threw an unexploded shell off his ship, which exploded in midair, injuring him.

In October, 1943, Hubbard was assigned to take a six-week course at the Naval Small Craft Training Center at Terminal Island in San Pedro, California. He was subsequently made navigating officer of the USS *Algol*.

In January, he wrote this depressed entry in his personal journal:

> My salvation is to let this
> roll over me, to write, write, and
> write some more. To hammer
> keys until I am finger worn to the
> second joint and then to hammer
> keys some more. To pile up copy,
> stack up stories, roll the
> wordage, and generally conduct
> my life along the one line of
> success I have ever had.[30]

As the *Algol* prepared to go into battle in the Pacific Theater, Hubbard applied for transfer to the School of Military Government at Princeton University. Although the transfer was approved, in a strange incident that occurred just before the *Algol* sailed to the Pacific, Hubbard discovered a homemade gasoline bomb in a Coke bottle amid the cargo being loaded on the ship. There was an investigation into this curious incident, but the results weren't recorded.

However, that evening, Hubbard was relieved from duty and sent to Princeton, where he completed a four-month training course.

In September, 1945, Hubbard was transferred to Monterrey, California, for further training. He reported in sick with a suspected ulcer and was hospitalized at Oak

---

[30] Ibid, p. 107

Knoll Military Hospital in Oakland, California, where he remained until December 5, 1945, when he was discharged from the Navy.

Contrary to his own report of receiving twenty-one war medals, he received four routine medals that were awarded to all servicemen serving in the war.

As soon as he was released from the Navy, Hubbard, again without any immediate financial prospects, began a series of requests to the Navy to award him a disability pension for injuries and ailments he claimed he sustained during the war. Among the complaints he listed were a sprained knee, an ulcer, conjunctivitis, arthritis, and malaria.

He was eventually awarded a small, partial disability rating, and his efforts to have that allowance increased continued for several years. In a pathetic letter to the Veteran's Administration dated October 15, 1947, Hubbard wrote:

> This is a request for treatment.
>
> After trying and failing for two years to regain my equilibrium in civil life, I am utterly unable to approach anything like my own competence. My last physician informed me that it might be helpful if I were to be examined and perhaps treated psychologically or even by a psychoanalyst. Toward the end of my service, I avoided, out of pride, any mental examinations, hoping that time would balance a mind which I had every reason to suppose was seriously affected. I

cannot account for nor rise above long periods of moroseness and suicidal inclinations, and have newly come to realize that I must first triumph above this before I can hope to rehabilitate myself at all.

I cannot leave school or what little work I am doing for hospitalization due to many obligations, but I feel I might be treated outside, possibly with success. I cannot, myself, afford such treatment.

Would you please help me?

Sincerely, L. Ron Hubbard[31]

After being discharged from the Navy in December, 1945, Hubbard didn't head for home, where Polly and his children still lived in Bremerton, Washington. Instead, he headed directly for a house in Pasadena, California, which housed an interesting, eclectic assortment of people, including Jack Parsons, leader of a satanic organization called the Ordo Templis Orientis, the US name for the organization headed in England by Aleister Crowley, the infamous black magician.

So began a new chapter in Hubbard's life, although, in actuality, it was but the continuation of an old one that began, reportedly, when Hubbard as a teen went to the Library of Congress with his mother and discovered a work written by Crowley.

Thereafter, he was fascinated by Crowley's *magick,* and Crowley became a mentor for Hubbard, a relationship that lasted until Crowley's death in 1947. In one of his later lectures, Hubbard referred to Crowley as "my good friend."

---

[31] Plaintiff's exhibit #336

Crowley's most famous work was *The Book of the Law,* in which he expressed his philosophy of life: *Do what thou wilt shall be the whole of the Law.* Hubbard was to live by that philosophy throughout his life.

In *The Book of the Law,* Crowley wrote:

> We have nothing with the outcast and the unfit: let them die in their misery. For they feel not. Compassion is the vice of Kings: stamp down the wretched and the weak: this is the law of the strong: this is our law and the joy of the world.
>
> I am of the snake that giveth Knowledge and Delight, and stirs the hearts of men with drunkenness. To worship me take wine and strange drugs.... They shall not harm ye at all. It is a lie, this folly against self.... Be strong, Oh man! Lust, enjoy all things of sense and rapture...the kings of the earth shall be kings forever: the slaves shall serve.
>
> Them that seek to entrap thee, to overthrow thee, them attack without pity or quarter; and destroy them utterly.
>
> I am unique and conqueror. I am not of the slaves that perish. Be they damned and dead! Amen.
>
> Pity not the fallen! I never knew them. I am not for them. I console not: I hate the consoled

and the consoler![32]

Perhaps this explains why, in Scientology, sympathy is considered a "low-toned" emotion. Scientologists learn in their training not to feel sympathy.

> According to Ron
> (Hubbard) Jr., his father
> considered himself to be the one
> "who came after"; that he was
> Crowley's successor; that he had
> taken on the mantle of the "Great
> Beast." He told him that
> Scientology actually began on
> December the 1st, 1947. This was
> the day Aleister Crowley died.[33]

Following in Crowley's footsteps, Hubbard adopted some of the practices of the black magician, including the use of drugs and the use of affirmations.

According to Hubbard's son, his father regularly used illegal drugs, including amphetamines, barbiturates, and hallucinogens, including cocaine, peyote, and mescaline.[34] Also, according to Hubbard, Jr., his father occasionally put Phenobarbital in his son's bubble gum.

Among the many affirmations that Hubbard was known to have used was the following:

> All men shall be my slaves!
> All women shall succumb to my
> charms! All mankind shall grovel
> at my feet and not know why![35]

---

[32] Corydon, p. 49

[33] Ibid, p. 50

[34] Ibid, p. 53

[35] Ibid, p. 53

Hubbard and Parsons struck up an occult partnership, the result of which was a series of rituals they carried out with the objective of producing a "moonchild," an incarnation of "Babylon" in an unborn child. A woman in the house was chosen to be the mother of this satanic child.

> During these rituals, which took place on the first three days of March, 1946, Parsons was the High Priest and had sexual intercourse with the girl, while Hubbard, who was present, acted as skryer, seer, or clairvoyant and described what was supposed to be happening on the astral plane.[36]

Later, Hubbard was to reveal some of his occult beliefs to his son in a conversation documented by L. Ron Hubbard, Jr.:

> "I've made the Magick really work," he (Hubbard, Sr.) says. "No more foolish rituals. I've stripped the Magick to basics—access without liability.
>
> "Sex by will," he says. "Love by will—no caring and no sharing—no feelings. None. Love reversed. Love isn't sex. Love is no good; puts you at effect. Sex is the route to power. Scarlet women! They are the secret to the doorway. Use and consume. Feast. Drink the power through them. Waste and discard them."
>
> "Scarlet?" I (Hubbard, Jr.,)

---

36 Ibid, p. 163

ask.

"Yes, Scarlet: the blood of
their bodies; the blood of their
souls.

"Release your will from
bondage. Bend their bodies; bend
their minds; bend their wills;
beat back the past. The present
is all there is. No consequences
and no guilt. Nothing is wrong in
the present. The will is free—
totally free; no feelings; no effort;
pure thought—separated. The
Will postulating the Will.

"Will, Sex, Love, Blood,
Door, Power, Will. Logical.

"The Doorway of Plenty.
The Great Door of the Great
Beast."[37]

The final result of the relationship between Hubbard
and Parsons was that Hubbard ran off with Parsons'
girlfriend, Sara Northrup, to Florida, where, with $20,000
of Parsons' money, they bought several boats and were
enjoying an easy life together at sea before Parsons
caught up with them and obtained a restraining order to
retrieve some of his assets.

On August 10, 1946, Hubbard and Sara were
married in Washington, DC, despite the fact that he was
still married to Polly. Sara didn't know about the existing
marriage to Polly or about Hubbard's two children.

Hubbard and Sara ended up living in a trailer in Port
Orchard, Washington, a few miles from Polly and the two
children in Bremerton, whom he visited occasionally. One
year and four months after he married Sara, his divorce

---

[37] Ibid, p. 307

from his first wife was granted. In April, 1950, just before the publication of *Dianetics: The Modern Science of Mental Health,* Hubbard became a father for the third time to Alexis, his daughter with Sara.

Unfortunately, his marriage to Sara was also fated to end in failure. Toward the end of their marriage, both Hubbard and Sara became involved in extramarital affairs.

Sara left Hubbard early in 1951, accusing him of being "paranoid schizophrenic." Hubbard, perhaps having a legitimate worry in that regard, retaliating by first kidnapping Alexis from the Church of Scientology premises in Los Angeles, then by kidnapping Sara and trying to have her declared insane in order to prevent her from doing the same to him.

Sara, in her divorce complaint, alleged that Hubbard had "repeatedly subjected her to systematic torture, including loss of sleep, beatings, and strangulations and scientific torture experiments." According to Sara, when Hubbard realized that a divorce was inevitable, he asked Sara to kill herself, fearing a divorce would ruin his reputation.

She said that Hubbard kept her from sleep for four days, then gave her sleeping pills, which nearly killed her. Once when he nearly strangled her, he ruptured the Eustachian tube in her ear, permanently impairing her hearing.

There were other allegations, and the conclusion reached in the divorce complaint was that Hubbard was "hopelessly insane."[38]

Hubbard fled to Cuba with baby Alexis, who was then nearly one year old. Eventually, after moving to Wichita to establish the Wichita Foundation with financier Don Purcell, Hubbard reached a settlement with Sara in which

---

[38] Ibid, p. 282

he agreed to return Alexis if Sara would recant her accusations against him.

On June 12, 1951, Sara traveled to Wichita to collect Alexis, signing a statement prepared by Hubbard that stated that the things she said about him were untrue, and that L. Ron Hubbard "is a fine and brilliant man."[39]

She caught a bus back to Los Angeles with baby Alexis and never saw Hubbard again.

Hubbard, meanwhile, carried on an affair with a student from the Wichita Foundation, a dark, pretty young Texan named Mary Sue Whipp. In March, 1952, Hubbard married Mary Sue, who was two months pregnant at the time of their wedding. She was his third and final wife, by whom he eventually had four more children.

From reports of people who were close to the family, although Mary Sue was devoted to her husband, Hubbard didn't develop close relationships with any of his seven children. His only interest in them was in what they could do to advance his interests in Scientology. When he learned of his son, Quentin's, suicide in October, 1976, he was heard to shout at the top of his voice, "That stupid fucking kid! That stupid fucking kid! Look what he's done to me...."[40]

Descriptions of Hubbard in the early fifties portray a man of contrasts. He could be charming when he wished, and, at other times, he could explode in outbursts of temper.

According to one student:

> Ron lectured every day. He
> was very impressive, dedicated,
> and amusing. The man had

---

[39] Ibid, p. 192

[40] Miller, p. 344

> tremendous charisma; you just
> wanted to hear every word he
> had to say and listen for any
> pearl of wisdom....[41]

Another student said:

> Hubbard has this
> incredible dynamism, a
> disarming, magnetic, and
> overwhelming personality. I
> remember being at Saint Hill one
> evening and running into him
> and as we started to talk, people
> gathered round. People had a
> wonderful feeling with him of
> being in the presence of a great
> man.[42]

Another student commented on Hubbard's unpredictability:

> He (Hubbard) could be very
> thoughtful and kind one minute
> and quite hideous the next. We
> were auditing about fifty hours a
> week and I remember one
> afternoon a girl burst into tears
> when she was telling Ron about a
> particularly difficult case she
> had. He put his arm around her
> and said, "Jenny, anything we
> can do for this preclear is better
> than doing nothing. She needs
> help and a bit of attention, and
> that's what you're giving her.
> Just keep on doing the same

---

[41] Ibid, p. 159

[42] Ibid, p. 252

thing you're doing, and you'll resolve it in due course. You can't expect miracles overnight."

That struck me as a very humane and comforting thing to say to her.... But then I have also seen him behave in a grotesque fashion. One afternoon during a lecture, a woman in the audience was coughing rather badly, and he walked to the front of the stage, red-faced and visibly angry, and shouted, "Get that woman out of this lecture hall!"

She was one of his most fervent supporters and was also desperately ill—she died three weeks later of lung cancer.[43]

Another aspect of Hubbard's character was his paranoia, a trait clearly evident in a series of lengthy letters he wrote to the FBI, accusing most of the associates working with him of being Communists who were plotting to destroy him. At one point, he wrote to the FBI accusing his wife, Sara, and her boyfriend of being Communists, a move with potentially dangerous consequences during the era of McCarthyism. Fortunately for the many people he named in those letters, the FBI didn't take Hubbard seriously, at one point making the notation *appears mental* in his file.

One of Hubbard's girlfriends during his marriage to Sara wrote about him:

He didn't trust anyone and was highly paranoid. He thought the CIA had hit men after him. We'd be walking along the street,

---

[43] Ibid, p. 224

> and I would ask, "Why are you
> walking so fast?"
>
> He would look over his
> shoulder and said, "You don't
> know what it's like to be a
> target."
>
> No one was after him; it
> was all delusion.[44]

Once, on an airplane trip with one of his staff
members, when the plane stopped for refueling, Hubbard
"scurried across the passenger terminal and stood with
his back pressed against a wall for the duration of the
stop, explaining to his companions that there were
people, 'Out to get him.'"[45]

During his late fifties and early sixties, Hubbard's
delusions seemed to become even more bizarre. In a
bulletin written in February, 1957, called *The Story of a
Static* (static being another Scientology term for the
thetan, or soul) Hubbard wrote:

> Once upon a time there
> was a thetan, and he was a
> happy little thetan, and the world
> was a simple thing. It was all
> very, very simple.
>
> And then one day,
> somebody told him he was
> simple.
>
> And ever since that time,
> he has been trying to prove that
> he is not.
>
> And that is the history of
> the Universe, the Human Race,

---

[44] Ibid, p. 166

[45] Ibid, p. 244

the Fifth Invaders, the Fourth
Invaders, the 3½ Invaders, the
people on Mars, Saturn, Jupiter,
Arcturus, the Marcab Galaxy, the
Marcab System, and Psi Galaxy,
Galaxy 82—

I don't care where you
look—that's the story.[46]

In another bulletin dated May 11, 1963, Hubbard
claimed he had twice visited heaven, 43 trillion and 42
trillion years earlier. Teaching his followers that heaven
was just an implant station in space, he said that on the
first visit, he found heaven "complete with gates, angels,
and plaster saints—and electronic implantation
equipment."

On his second visit, one trillion years later, he said
that he found changes in heaven.

The place is shabby. The
vegetation is gone. The pillars are
scruffy. The saints have
vanished. So have the angels. A
sign on one side (the left as you
enter) says, *This is Heaven.* The
right has a sign *Hell* with an
arrow and inside the grounds one
can see archaeological diggings
with terraces that lead to "Hell."
Plain wire fencing encloses the
place....[47]

In one of the tapes on the Saint Hill Special Briefing
Course, Hubbard claims to have been flying around space
without his body, getting caught in the Van Allen Belt,
and he related this experience in great detail for his

---

[46] Professional Auditor's Bulletin No. 105

[47] Miller, p. 247-9

students. Later, in the Sea Org, a student on the ship related this experience with Hubbard:

> LRH (Hubbard) was on the ship and in a real jolly mood. He used to stay up late at night on the deck and talk to us into the wee hours about his whole track (past life) adventures, how he was a racecar driver in the Marcab civilization.
>
> The Marcab civilization existed millions of years ago on another planet; it was similar to planet earth in the fifties, only they had space travel.... (Hubbard) said he was a race driver called the Green Dragon, who set a speed record before he was killed in an accident. He came back in another lifetime as the Red Devil and beat his own record, then came back and did it again as the Blue Streak.
>
> People would stand around listening to these stories for hours, very overawed. At the time, it seemed like a privilege and an honor to share these things, to hear him talking about things that went on millions of years ago like it was yesterday.[48]

Hubbard should probably have been diagnosed as a manic-depressive with paranoid tendencies, according to several people who knew him well. Certainly, he had occasional periods of deep depression, in which he lay in

---

[48] Ibid, p. 279

bed in a torpor, once telling one of his attendants that he wanted to die.[49]

> "He developed phobias about dust and smells which were the cause of frequent explosive temper tantrums. He was always complaining that his clothes smelled of soap or he was being choked by dust that no one else could detect."

> On his trips between the ship and a rented villa in Las Palmas, "he would insist on stopping because there was dust in the air-conditioning. He would get into such a rage that on occasion I thought he was going to tear the car apart."[50]

His temper tantrums increased with age. After a motorcycle accident in Tenerife in the Canary Islands, in which he broke his arm and several ribs, he was in a particularly vile temper.

> "He didn't get out of that red chair for three months," Doreen Smith said, (one of his young aides in the Commodore's Messenger Organization). "He'd sleep for about forty-five minutes at a time, then be awake for hours, and screaming and shouting. It was impossible to get him comfortable. None of us got any sleep. I was better with a

---

[49] Ibid, p. 266

[50] Ibid, p. 267

cushion. Someone else was
better with a footstool, someone
else with cotton padding, so
every time he woke up, we all
had to be in there, fussing
around him while he was
screaming at us that we were all
'stupid fucking shitheads'...he
was out of control."[51]

According to another aide, after the accident at Tenerife, conditions about the ship took a turn for the worse:

"His actions definitely
became more bizarre after the
motorcycle accident. You could
hear him throughout the ship,
shouting, ranting and raving day
after day. He was always
claiming that the cooks were
trying to poison him, and he
began to smell odors everywhere.
His clothes had to be washed in
pure water thirteen times, using
thirteen different buckets of
clean water to rinse a shirt, so he
wouldn't smell detergent on it.[52]

His young messengers bore the brunt of his temper throughout his later years, although they continued to serve him with devotion.

According to one Sea Org member who later defected:

His messengers were there
to cater to Hubbard's every need.

---

[51] Ibid, p. 320

[52] Ibid, p. 321

The girls would stick cigarettes in
his mouth and light them. They
had to catch his cigarette ashes.
If a drop of sweat was on his
forehead, they had to wipe it off.
Every word he said had to be
written down by the girls.
Whenever he appeared, people
would clap. If it was four in the
morning, and nobody could see
straight, people would clap.[53]

The girls in the Sea Org also served as his personal
attendants:

When he woke up, he
would yell, "Messenger," and two
of us would go into his room
straightaway. He would usually
be lying in his bunk in his
underwear with one arm
outstretched, waiting for us to
pull him up to a sitting position.

While one of us put a robe
around his shoulders, the other
one would give him a cigarette, a
Kool nonfilter, light it, and stand
ready with an ashtray. I would
run into the bathroom to make
sure his toothbrush, soap, and
razor were all laid out in a set
fashion, and I prepared his bath,
checked the shampoo, towel, and
temperature of the water.

When he went into the
bathroom, we would lay out his
clothes, powder his socks and

---

[53] Corydon, p. 175

shoes, and fold everything ready
to get him dressed. Everything
had to be right, because if it
wasn't, he would yell at us, and
we didn't want to upset him. The
last thing we wanted to do was
upset him.

When he came out of the
shower, he would be in his
underwear. Two of us held his
pants off the floor, as he stepped
into them. He didn't like the
trouser legs to touch the floor,
God forbid that should happen.

We pulled up his pants
and buckled his belt, although he
zipped them. We put on his shirt,
buttoned it up, put his Kools in
his shirt pocket, tied his cravat,
and combed his hair.

All this time, he'd be
standing there watching us run
around him. Then we'd follow
him out onto the deck carrying
anything he might need—cloak,
hat, binoculars, ashtray, spare
cigarettes, anything he could
possibly think of wanting. We felt
it was an honor and a privilege to
do anything for him.[54]

Once someone asked what inspired him to form the
CMO, Commodore's Messenger Organization:

He said it was an idea he
had picked up from Nazi
Germany. He said Hitler was a

---

[54] Miller, p. 322

madman, but nevertheless, a
genius in his own right, and the
Nazi Youth was one of the
smartest ideas he ever had. With
young people, you had a blank
slate, and you could write
anything you wanted on it, and it
would be your writing.

That was his idea, to take
young people and mold them into
little Hubbards. He said he had
girls, because women were more
loyal than men.[55]

According to some of the messengers, Hubbard didn't
have sex with them. One of the messengers stated, "I
think he got his thrills by just having us around."[56]

One reason for that was that Hubbard was reportedly
impotent. "It is documented that Hubbard used huge
amounts of testosterone, stilbestrol (a female sex
hormone). Taking the sex hormones was his solution to
an impotence problem."[57]

One woman with whom Hubbard did have a sexual
encounter described a very strange experience. She was
taken to a room in one of the Sea Org buildings in Los
Angeles, and described a man who fit Hubbard's
description:

Sitting on one of the
chairs...was a heavyset older
man. He had reddish gray hair,
slightly long in the back. He was
wearing a white shirt, black

---

[55] Ibid, p. 323

[56] Ibid, p. 323

[57] Corydon, p. 288

pants, black tie, and black shoes, highly polished....

He didn't say a word and slowly got up, motioned me to follow him into the next room. I found myself in a lavish bedroom....

Without a word, he suddenly began to undress me. I was repelled by him. I didn't want to sleep with him, yet I felt really chilled and cold to the bone at that moment.

I acutely sensed real fear and danger in the room. In an instant, I realized the calculated power coming from this person. If I resisted, I knew that my punishment would be extreme.

His eyes were so blank, no emotion, no interaction, nothing was there.

I made the decision not to resist no matter what happened. I realized it would be a bad mistake for me to do so. He seemed to be completely divorced from reality. He was so strange that I realized that if I provoked him, he could be extremely dangerous.

I let him undress me without resisting. I was totally unprepared for what happened next.

He lay on top of me. As far as I can tell, he had no erection.

However, using his hand in some way, he managed to get his penis inside me. Then, for the next hour, he did absolutely nothing at all. I mean nothing!

After the first twenty-five minutes, I became about as frightened as I have ever been in my life. I felt as if in some perverse way, he was telling me that he hated me as a female. I then began to feel that my mind was being ripped away from me by force.

That was the worst of it all. I really felt he coveted an aspect of my personality, and he wanted it. This was weird, total control on a level I could not fathom at the time. I had no idea what was happening.

After half an hour, I really thought I was going crazy. I couldn't move my body from underneath him, and I could feel he still had no erection.

He wouldn't look at me, but instead kept his head averted to the side and just gazed into space.

I had to discipline myself to keep from screaming, because I felt I was having a nervous breakdown. Then I got the terrible thought that he was dead. He was hardly breathing. Then I thought he would kill me, too. My thoughts became very morbid.

After an hour, he got up
and walked out. I just lay there
for ten minutes. Then
mechanically I got dressed.
Instantly after that I began crying
hysterically. I cried and cried and
cried....

I didn't say a word to
anyone.[58]

After Quentin's death in 1976, Hubbard seemed to change. Before his son's suicide, he had been in rare good spirits, working with his messengers to produce movies.

But after Quentin's death, "He reverted to the familiar bellowing, foul-mouthed tyrant, plagued by phobias, surrounded by fools, and besieged by enemies."[59]

Hubbard was deteriorating in body as well as in mind and spirit. He's described by a messenger who met him for the first time in the desert in California during the late seventies:

The first night I was there,
I didn't talk to LRH (Hubbard),
since he was busy, but I saw
him. He had long, reddish-gray
hair down past his shoulders,
rotting teeth, and a really fat gut.
He didn't look anything like his
pictures.

The next day, I met him.
He was doing exercises in the
courtyard and called me over. I
was nervous meeting him. I was

---

[58] Ibid, p. 126

[59] Miller, p. 348

really surprised that I didn't feel
this "electric something-or-other"
that I was told happens when
you're around him.[60]

Another messenger working for him in the desert
said, describing her first meeting with Hubbard, that:

I was working in the
wardrobe department when I
heard a barrage of abuse from
behind a screen. "You dirty
goddamn sons of bitches, you're
so goddamn stupid. Fuck you,
cocksuckers...."

It seemed to go on for
several minutes. I asked, "Who in
the world is that?"

They said it was the Boss.
We weren't allowed to use the
name Hubbard for security
reasons.

"You mean the leader of
the church speaks like that?" I
asked.

"Oh, yes. He doesn't believe
in keeping anything back."[61]

But later, in hiding in Hemet, his mood once again
seemed to improve.

In the evenings, he would
reminisce to a small, but always
attentive, audience. He was a
good storyteller, and it was nice
to listen to him. He told us once

---

[60] Ibid, p. 348

[61] Ibid, p. 354

> how he was Tamburlaine's wife,
> and how he had wept when
> Tamburlaine was routed in his
> last great battle.
>
> Another time, he was on a
> disabled spaceship that landed
> here before life began and
> realized that potential and
> brought seeds back from another
> planet to fertilize planet
> earth....[62]

One young follower said that he recalled:

> sitting on the floor with a
> couple of messengers while
> (Hubbard) played hillbilly songs
> on his guitar and talked about
> the time he had earned his living
> as a troubadour in the Blue
> Mountains. I think he made up
> the songs as he went along....
> Afterward, everyone clapped.[63]

During his last five years, fearing discovery by federal officials, Hubbard went into even-deeper seclusion retiring with three trusted messengers to a secret ranch in Creston, California. In a final glimpse, a man named Robert Whaley said that Hubbard could be seen:

> puttering around in baggy
> blue pants and a yellow straw
> hat, taking photographs. He was
> overweight, and, with his white
> hair and white beard, reminded
> Whaley of Kentucky Fried
> Chicken's Colonel Sanders.

---

[62] Ibid, p. 362

[63] Ibid, p. 362

> Once Whaley walked
> across to (the ranch) to see if he
> could borrow a tool and
> surprised the old man in the
> stable. (Hubbard) was busy filing
> a piece of metal and was
> evidently not pleased to see his
> neighbor; he glared suspiciously
> at Whaley for a second, then
> scurried off into a workshop
> without a word, locking the door
> behind him.[64]

To his followers, Hubbard was the Messiah and the reincarnation of Buddha. In a poem called *Hymn of Asia,* he told them:

> Everywhere you are I can
> be addressed
>
> But in your temples best
>
> Address me and you
> address Lord Buddha
>
> Address Lord Buddha
>
> And then you address
> Meitreya.[65]

On January 24, 1986, Hubbard died at his ranch in Creston of a cerebral hemorrhage. He was cremated and his ashes scattered at sea.

On January 27, his followers gathered at the Hollywood Paladium in Los Angeles for a briefing by the new head of Scientology, Hubbard's protégé, David Miscavige. Miscavige announced that Hubbard had gone of to "his next level of research," a level done in a state exterior to the body:

---

[64] Ibid, p. 373

[65] Corydon, p. 15

Thus, at 2000 hours, Friday, 24 January, 1986, L. Ron Hubbard discarded the body he had used in this lifetime for seventy-four years, ten months, and eleven days. The body he had used to facilitate his existence in this universe had ceased to be useful, and, in fact, had become an impediment to the work he now must do outside its confines.

The being we knew as L. Ron Hubbard still exists. Although you may feel grief, understand that he did not and does not now. He has simply moved on to his next step. (Hubbard) in fact used this lifetime and body we knew to accomplish what no man has ever accomplished—he unlocked the mysteries of life and gave us the tools so we could free ourselves and our fellow men.[66]

Hubbard left most of his immense fortune to the Church of Scientology. For his funeral service, Hubbard wrote his own eulogy:

And so we send into the chain of all-enduring time our heritage, our hope, our friend. Good-bye, Ron. Your people thank you for having lived. Earth is a better place for your having lived.

---

[66] Miller, p. 375

We thank you for coming
to us. We do not contest your
right to go away. Your debts are
paid. This chapter of thy life is
shut. Go now, dear Ron, and live
once more in happier time and
place. Thank you, Ron.

And now here lift up your
eyes and say to him, "Good-bye.
Good-bye, our dear. Good-bye.
We'll miss you, you know...."

Come, Friends. He's all
right. And he's gone. We have our
work to do, and he has his. He
will be welcome there. To man.[67]

L. Ron Hubbard is gone, but he left behind the legacy
of his church, with its 100,000 dedicated members,
working fervently to carry his dream of a "cleared planet"
and a "new and better civilization" to the rest of the world.

To study a man like Hubbard demands a study of the
nature of evil. Hubbard was faithful to the credo of his
mentor, Aleister Crowley, which was, "Do as thou wilt."
Hubbard lived by no laws but his own.

There is an interesting story that once one of
Hubbard's associates told him, "It would be nice if we
could be closer friends," to which Hubbard replied, "Yes,
it would be nice, but I can't have any friends."[68]

Hubbard was a psychological vampire. People existed
for him to exploit—their time, energy, and assets sucked
out and used to his profit.

Hubbard scorned his followers, refusing to be called a
Scientologist in much the same way that a Scientologist

[67] From a tape of the funeral service

[68] Miller, p. 218

scorns the label of "wog," refusing to be identified with the lower life forms outside Scientology. ("Wog" being the Scientology designation for a nonScientologist.)

There are signs, however, that Hubbard, "Source," had in the end fallen victim to his own trap. In the later days of his life, he continued to audit himself daily in search of the elusive freedom he had packaged and marketed so successfully to others.

Hubbard, undoubtedly a genius, was most human at certain points in his life when he was able to admit to his vulnerabilities. One such moment was his letter written in the Navy, in which he lamented his tendency to fail at everything but his writing, "the one line of success I have ever had."[69]

Another instance was his 1947 letter to the Veteran's Administration, begging for psychiatric help. "Would you please help me?" he ends that pathetic letter, a call for help that apparently went unanswered. One can only wonder what the outcome might have been had he received that help. It's possible that his thousands of victims might have been spared. It's even possible that his formidable genius, channeled into a more positive direction, might have resulted in some more laudable achievement in the field of the mind.

Hubbard is gone, but his church—Scientology—lives on as the externalization of Hubbard's paranoia. We have only too recently seen the effect that one madman can have on history and the lives of millions. In the end, the success or failure of Scientology will depend on the inhabitants of the "wog" world, and whether they are willing to trade their freedom and sensibilities for the elusive promises of Scientology.

---

[69] Ibid, p. 108

CHAPTER THREE

The Propaganda of Scientology—
"Playing for Blood"

When you have succeeded in making men believe that change is necessary and possible and that they are the ones who can achieve it; when you have convinced them that they and the small minority of whom they are a part can transform the world in their lifetime, you have achieved something very considerable indeed. You have put into their lives a dynamic force so powerful that you can bring them to do what would otherwise be impossible. The dull and humdrum becomes meaningful. Life becomes purposeful and immensely more worth living.

Douglas Hyde, *Dedication and Leadership*

Douglas Hyde, the author quoted above, was for twenty years a dedicated Communist and the news editor of the London edition of the *Daily Worker,* a Communist newspaper.

Becoming disillusioned with the inconsistencies he saw between the stated ideology of the Communist Party and the translation of that ideology into actual practice,

Hyde rejected the Party, resigned his job, and eventually became converted to the Catholic Church. In 1966, he delivered a series of lectures to a convocation of Catholic leaders from at least five continents, and the book *Dedication and Leadership* consists of transcripts from those lectures.

In the first lecture, Hyde stated:

> If you ask me what is the distinguishing mark of the Communist, what it is that Communists most outstandingly have in common, I would say...that beyond any shadow of doubt it is their idealism, their zeal, dedication, devotion to their cause, and willingness to sacrifice.... The vast majority of the Communists I have met anywhere conform to this pattern.[70]

This same quote is equally true if read with the word *Scientologist* substituted for the word *Communist*. This is also true of the following paragraph from the same lecture:

> Youth is a period of idealism. The Communists [Scientologists] attract young people by appealing directly to that idealism. Too often, others have failed either to appeal to it or to use it, and they are the losers as a consequence. We have no cause to complain, if, having neglected the idealism of youth, we see others come along, take it,

---

[70] Hyde, p. 15

> use it, and harness it to their
> cause—against our own.[71]

Nowhere is there a group of predominantly young people more idealistic, more dedicated, more fervently devoted to their cause than in Scientology. Scientologists give their all—their time, energy, money, assets, and even their children—to the cause, frequently living in a manner that would seem comfortably familiar to, for example, a first-century Christian.

The fanatic dedication of the Scientologist doesn't happen by accident. It's carefully and systematically inculcated by the propaganda of Scientology, to which both the novice and seasoned Scientologists are exposed on a daily basis. Essential, therefore, to understanding both Scientology and the Scientologist is an examination of the propaganda contained in the millions of words of Hubbard on tape recordings and in printed "bulletins" listened to or read daily by the Scientologist.

A distinction is made here between the propaganda of Scientology and that of Dianetics. In Dianetics, the new convert is led to believe in cures for an endless array of physical maladies, from asthma to allergies to cancer, and even to believe that through Dianetic and Scientology auditing there will be an exemption from death itself. It's fabled that through auditing, the Scientologist of advanced age will be able to simply "drop the body" at will and without pain.

But it is through the propaganda of Scientology, separate from the subscience of Dianetics, that the true programming of the Scientologist takes place. It operates as follows:

Upon entry into Scientology, the initiate is given a packet of written materials consisting of a series of

---

[71] Ibid, p. 17

printed "bulletins" by Hubbard and serving as an introduction into the sect.

One of the first bulletins the initiate reads is titled, *The Aims of Scientology*. This bulletin is important, because it delivers the very first message to the newcomer, the message that Scientology is a Good Thing:

A civilization without insanity, without criminals, and without war, where the able can prosper and honest beings can have rights, and where Man is free to rise to greater heights, are the aims of Scientology.

First announced to the enturbulated world fifteen years ago, these aims are well within the grasp of our technology.

Nonpolitical in nature, Scientology welcomes any individual of any creed, race, or nation.

We seek no revolution. We seek only evolution to higher states of being for the individual and for Society.

We are achieving our aims.

After endless millennia of ignorance about himself, his mind, and the Universe, a breakthrough has been made for Man.

Other efforts Man has made have been surpassed.

The combined truths of fifty thousand years of thinking men, distilled and amplified by new discoveries about Man, have made for this success.

We welcome you to Scientology. We only expect of you your help in achieving our aims and helping others. We expect you to be helped.

Scientology is the most vital movement on Earth today.

In a turbulent world, the job is not easy. But then, if it were, we wouldn't have to be doing it.

We respect Man and believe he is worthy of help. We respect you and believe you, too, can help.

Scientology does not owe its help. We have done nothing to cause us to propitiate. Had we done so, we would not now be bright enough to do what we are doing.

Man suspects all offers of help. He has often been betrayed, his confidence shattered. Too frequently, he has given his trust and been betrayed. We may err, for we build a world with broken straws. But we will never betray your faith in us so long as you are one of us.

The sun never sets on Scientology.

And may a new day dawn on you, for those you love, and for Man.

Our aims are simple, if

great.

And we will succeed, and
are succeeding at each new
revolution of the Earth.

Your help is acceptable to
us.

Our help is yours.

L. Ron Hubbard, Founder

Similarly, in the next bulletin the newcomer to Scientology will read, called *My Philosophy*, he or she receives the message that the founder of Scientology, L. Ron Hubbard, is a good and wise man:

The first principle of my
own philosophy is that wisdom is
meant for anyone who wishes to
reach for it. It is the servant of
the commoner and king alike and
should never be regarded with
awe....

The second principle of my
own philosophy is that it must be
capable of being applied....

The third principle is that
any philosophic knowledge is
only valuable or true if it
works....

A philosophy can only be a
route to knowledge. It cannot be
crammed down one's throat. If
one has a route, he can then find
what is true for him. And that is
Scientology.

Know Thyself...and the
truth shall set you free....

I like to help others and
count it as my greatest pleasure

in life to see a person free himself of the shadows which darken his days....

I have seen much human misery. As a very young man, I wandered through Asia and saw the agony and misery of overpopulated and underdeveloped lands. I have seen people uncaring and stepping over dying men in the streets. I have seen children less than rags and bones. And amongst this poverty and degradation, I found holy places where wisdom was great, but where it was carefully hidden and given out only as superstition.

Later, in Western universities, I saw Man obsessed with materiality, and with all his cunning, I saw him hide what little wisdom he really had in forbidding halls and make it inaccessible to the common and less-favored man. I have been through a terrible war and saw its terror and pain uneased by a single word of decency of humanity.

I have lived no cloistered life and hold in contempt the wise man who has not lived and the scholar who will not share.

There have been many wiser men than I, but few have traveled as much road.

I have seen life from the
top down and the bottom up. I
know how it looks both ways.
And I know there is wisdom and
that there is hope.

But I have never seen
wisdom do any good kept to
oneself, and, as I like to see
others happy, and as I find the
vast majority of the people can
and do understand, I will keep on
writing and working and teaching
as long as I exist.

For I know no man who
has any monopoly upon the
wisdom of this universe. It
belongs to those who can use it
to help themselves and others.

If things were a little better
known and understood, we
would all lead happier lives.

And there is a way to know
them, and there is a way to
freedom.

The old must give way to
the new, falsehood must become
exposed by truth, and truth,
though fought, always in the end
prevails.

L. Ron Hubbard

In all of the propaganda of Scientology, four lessons
predominate:

1. That there is a problem.

2. That there is a solution to the problem.

3. That the solution can only be found in
Scientology.

4. What will happen if the problem isn't solved.

The first problem posed by Hubbard is the imminent danger of nuclear war, and only Scientology has the potential to thwart this danger:

> We are the only people and the only organization on Earth which have the technology and the ambition to attempt a clarification of situations which, in other hands, are considered entirely out of control, to wit, the atomic bomb and the decay and confusion of central governments.
>
> From *Purpose,* by L. Ron Hubbard
>
> The use or neglect of this material [Scientology] may well determine the use or neglect of the atomic bomb by Man.... In the same period of history, two of the most sweeping forces Man has known have come to fruition: a knowledge of himself and others with Scientology, and a means of destroying himself and all others by atomic fission. Which force wins depends in a large measure on your use of Scientology.
>
> The mission of Scientology is not conquest—it is civilization. It is a war upon stupidity, the stupidity which leads us to the Last War of All.
>
> As your associates, their homes, their children, their

possessions, and all their futures lie ending in a radioactive street, there won't be time to wish we'd worked harder, been less easily dissuaded from pressing our arguments....

There is not much Earth time in which to distribute this knowledge. This is the solution to our barbarism out of which we would lose all.... It is time Man grew up. This is what we have in mind. For there can be but weeping in the night where ignorance, factionalism, hatred, and exploitation are served by the most ferocious and final weapon of all—the H-bomb.

With man now equipped with weapons sufficient to destroy all mankind on Earth, the emergence of a new science capable of handling man is vital. Scientology is such a science.... With Scientology, man can prevent insanity, criminality, and war.... The primary race of Earth is not between one nation and another today. The only race that matters at this moment is the one being run between Scientology and the atomic bomb. The history of man, as has been said by well-known historians, may well depend upon which one wins.

From *Fundamentals of Thought* by L. Ron Hubbard

The second problem posed by Hubbard is that mankind is caught in a trap and has been in it for millions of years, during which he has been recycling back to Earth through an endless series of lifetimes. It's only through Scientology auditing that he can escape that trap:

> In fifty thousand years of history on this planet alone, Man never evolved a workable system. It is doubtful if, in foreseeable history, he will ever evolve another.
>
> Man is caught in a huge and complex labyrinth. To get out of it requires that he follow the closely taped path of Scientology.
>
> Scientology will take him out of the labyrinth. But only if he follows the exact markings in the tunnels.
>
> It has taken me a third of a century in this lifetime to tape this route out.
>
> From *Safeguarding Techniques* by L. Ron Hubbard
>
> We're free men and women—probably the last free men and women on Earth.... If we don't do a good job now, we may never get another chance.
>
> So we have an organization, we have a chance.
>
> That's more than we had last time night's curtain began to fall on freedom.
>
> An organization such as

ours is our best chance to get the
most done. So we're doing it!

From *Your Post* by L. Ron
Hubbard

Is there a way out?

Yes, there is.

We have it in Scientology
now. I have found it and charted
it. I know exactly how to open the
gate.

From *Escape* by L. Ron
Hubbard

The whole agonized future
of this planet, every Man,
Woman, and Child on it, and
your own destiny for the next
endless trillions of years depends
on what you do here and now
with and in Scientology.

From *Keeping Scientology
Working,* by L. Ron Hubbard

The Scientologist is trained to believe that the
salvation of mankind can only be achieved by the
"science" of Scientology, and that Scientology supercedes
any other mental health technology. There is no other
hope:

In all the broad universe
there is no other hope for man
than ourselves.

From *Ron's Journal 1967,*
by L. Ron Hubbard

Let us face the reality of
this thing. The world confronts
several crises. Man's inhumanity
to Man is gaining monuments
daily. The time to bring a chaos

under control is before it is well begun. We're slightly late as it is. Brutally, there is no other organization on Earth that can slow these down. Factually, there is no other know-how on Earth that can plumb the problems of Man. So if we don't want all of us to be sitting amongst the charred embers, we had better get busy.

From *The Eighteenth A.C.C.* by L. Ron Hubbard

We are the first group on earth that knew what they were talking about. All right, sail in. The world's ours. Own it.

From *The World Is Ours* by L. Ron Hubbard

Auditors have since the first session of Scientology been the only individuals on this planet in this universe capable of freeing Man.

From *Auditors* by L. Ron Hubbard

(Scientology) is the only valid and fully tested mental process which Man has.

From *The Road Up* by L. Ron Hubbard

Scientology is a science of life. It is the first entirely Western effort to understand life. All earlier efforts came from Asia or Eastern Europe. And they failed.... Scientology is something new under the sun, but young as it is, it is still the only completely and thoroughly tested and validated science of existence.

From *The Problems of Work* by L. Ron Hubbard

Scientology, in less than a decade, has become the world's primary study of Man and the mind and has today more offices and practitioners than all other Nineteenth Century practices combined. Thus we must learn to bury the past of mental healing and look forward to our better day, the day of Scientology and new hope, the day of help without threat or harm, the day of a new and better civilization, born with the birth of a better understanding of Man.

From *What Scientology Is* by L. Ron Hubbard

Through their training, Scientologists learn that they are the true elite in this world, and that one cannot be a good Scientologist unless he or she is tough and dedicated:

We're the elite of Planet Earth....

From *Current Planning* by L. Ron Hubbard

When somebody enrolls [in Scientology], consider he or she has joined up for the duration of the universe—never permit an "open-minded" approach. If they're going to quit let them quit fast. If they enrolled, they're

aboard, and if they're aboard,
they're here on the same terms
as the rest of us—win or die in
the attempt. Never let them be
half-minded about being
Scientologists. The finest
organizations in history have
been tough, dedicated
organizations....

It's a tough universe. The
social veneer makes it seem mild.
But only the tigers survive—and
even they have a hard time. We'll
survive because we are tough
and are dedicated. When we do
instruct somebody properly he
becomes more and more tiger.
When we instruct half-mindedly
and are afraid to offend, scared
to enforce, we don't make
students into good Scientologists
and that lets everybody down.
When Mrs. Pattycake comes to
us to be taught, turn that
wandering doubt in her eye into
a fixed, dedicated glare, and
she'll win and we'll all win.
Humor her and we all die a little.

From *Keeping Scientology
Working* by L. Ron Hubbard

Douglas Hyde, Communist turned Catholic, lists as
one of the primary reasons for the success of Communist
teaching the fact that the subject is always presented in
global terms. That there is a global battle going on with
"suffering, sweating, toiling humanity" on one side and
the new Communist Man on the other.

Scientology is also presented to believers in global
terms as "The Road to Total Freedom" and as "The Only

Hope for Mankind." The goal of every Scientologist is nothing less than to "Clear the planet," to ensure the salvation of every person on earth through the attainment of the Scientology state of "Clear."

Salvation of mankind through Scientology is an endeavor of vital importance and with global implications:

We're playing for blood, the stake is EARTH.

From Policy Letter of 7 Nov., 1962, of L. Ron Hubbard

The purpose of the Field Staff Member [Scientologist] is:

To help LRH [Hubbard] contact, handle, salvage, and bring understanding to individuals and thus the peoples of Earth.

From *Field Auditors* by L. Ron Hubbard

Now, without further discourse, let's get hot. This is Scientology—the freedom for Man. Let it be known.

From *The Public Divisions* by L. Ron Hubbard

The Valuable Final Products of a Scientologist are:

DISSEMINATED KNOWLEDGE

PURCHASED BOOKS

ENVIRONMENTAL CONTROL

A CLEARED PLANET

From *Org Board Division Size* by L. Ron Hubbard

The witch and the pot; the
test tube and the scope; the cell
and the club; the textbook and
the lies—Control! Control them
or we die! Beat them or they win!
Starve them or we shrink. We are
afraid! Afraid! Afraid!—They said
that in the old age we killed.

Freedom becks and we now
laughing at their lives, went free.

Scientology—The Road
Sign Out.

We are the Free People. We
LIVE! We're FREE!

From *We Are the Free
People* by L. Ron Hubbard

My purpose is to bring a
barbarism out of the mud it
thinks conceived it and to form
here on Earth a civilization based
on human understanding, not
violence.

That's a big purpose. A
broad field. A star-high goal.

But I think it's your
purpose, too.

From *How We Work on the
Third Dynamic* by L. Ron
Hubbard

We are the prime movers in
this, the new age. Forget the old.
Face up to what will come. And
let the dead yesterdays bury the
philosophical Authority and
Capital Gains and Communist
psychology cults. We're no longer
tied.

The eons march on....
Perhaps, this time, due to our
efforts, a humanitarian world can
exist. We, the Prophets of the
Morrow, know the way.

From *Scientology: The
Philosophy of a New Age* by L.
Ron Hubbard

There is no greater game in
the Universe than Scientology,
for it is the only game in which
everybody wins.

From *Contests and Prizes*
by L. Ron Hubbard

We are the people who are
ending the cycle of homo sapiens
and starting the cycle of the good
earth.

There is no barrier on our
path except those we make
ourselves.

Our ability belongs to all
worlds everywhere.

From *What Is Scientology?*
by L. Ron Hubbard

The excerpts given in this chapter are only a small
sampling of the propaganda to which a Scientologist is
exposed on a daily basis. The fact that exposure to such
propaganda comes immediately after one has done a
series of hypnotic, mind-numbing drills known as
"training routines" serves only to render the propaganda
more deeply ingrained and more ferociously grasped by
the Scientologist.

These beliefs, instilled in the mind of a Scientologist
through endless hours of listening to the rambling, tape-
recorded lectures of Hubbard, or through the volumes of
printed bulletins that are required reading on the many

"courses" or classes in Scientology, soon take precedence over any prior system of belief.

Within a relatively short time, Scientology is able to produce a fully programmed, doctrine-espousing, bulletin-believing, fanatic Scientologist whose mind is lost behind the steel trap of cult programming, impervious to the logic and pleadings of well-intentioned family or friends.

Is there such a thing as thought control? Is it really possible for a mind to be brought under the full control of another?

Ask any ex-Scientologist or a fugitive from any other cult. He will tell you that the answer is an incontrovertible, "Yes." Our minds are programmed from birth by parents, teachers, friends, books, movies, and commercials on radio and TV, but nowhere are the results of programming more insidious than in a cult like Scientology.

Parents desperate to "rescue" their child from the grasp of a mind-bending cult like Scientology find themselves impotent in the face of a legal system without meaningful precedents in the gray area of mind control. It is illegal for them to kidnap their child to deprogram his twisted cult thinking. The fact that the child has already been kidnapped mentally by the cult is not, legally, a factor. Psychological kidnapping isn't a crime.

Perhaps the only remedy for those still in relative possession of their critical faculties is a warning:

Cherish your mind and guard it well. Beware the Hubbards of the world who seek to capture and harness your mind for their own predatory purposes.

For thousands of young people in this country and others, it's already too late.

CHAPTER FOUR

TRs the Hard Way—"Flunk for blinking! Start!"

Public courses on TRs are NOT "softened" because they are for the Public. Absolutely no standards are lowered. THE PUBLIC ARE GIVEN REAL TRS— ROUGH, TOUGH, AND HARD.... Comm Courses Are Not a Tea Party.

L. Ron Hubbard, Training Drills Modernized

The reeducation process begins with a person's most basic and important dealings—the interaction with other humans and the relationship to oneself. This undercuts any reeducation of American prisoners of war in North Korean concentration camps. Their reeducation was in terms of political loyalties. That was a light task compared to the revisions the Comm Course makes.

TR1 involves a relearning of how to talk; with TR2, a relearning of how to listen; with TR3, a relearning of how properly

to ask a question; and with TR4,
there is a relearning of how to
interact with another. The
student's regression to a childlike
and impressionable state is the
result.

Ford Schwartz, an ex-
Scientologist

One of the questions frequently asked of ex-Scientologists, usually by well-meaning but uninformed friends, goes something like this: "How could a smart person like you get into something as bizarre as Scientology?"

Unfortunately, there's no simple answer to that question. Involvement in Scientology comes about as a result of a complex interplay of several ill-defined, esoteric factors, such as mind control, thought reform, and social conditioning.

The process of indoctrination in Scientology is both ingenious and subtle. The initiate, believing himself to be on the "Road to Total Freedom" is drawn further and further into the trap.

A close examination of the process of Scientology reveals that there are within this carefully designed system of manipulation and control some characteristics common to all cults and other forms of mind control.

How does mind control within Scientology work? Let's take a look.

Within Scientology, a new person walking through the front door the first time is known as "raw meat." In other words, he's food for the sharks.

Usually, a person comes to Scientology for one of three reasons: he heard a testimony of a Scientologist friend or family member; he read the Dianetics book and became intrigued by its global promises; or he came in for a free personality test offered by many Scientology organizations as a means of attracting "raw meat."

Once inside the front door, the person may take the free personality test, see a movie, or sit through an introductory lecture. The end result of all three is the same. After the test, movie, or lecture, the newcomer will be interviewed by a Scientology "Registrar," whose job is to get the person registered—signed up and paid for—for his first "course" in Scientology. For most people, the first course and point of entry into Scientology is called the "Communication Course."

The way that the Registrar is trained to accomplish that task is very interesting. He knows that he must "find the ruin" of the newcomer seated across from him. That can be anything from shyness and inability to communicate, to marital problems, to addiction to a substance (drugs, alcohol, food, cigarettes), to a chronic physical problem, such as asthma or cancer.

The Registrar knows that once he has succeeded in finding that ruin, he has the magic ticket to get the person into Scientology.

If the person took the personality test, finding the ruin is easy by taking the lowest score on the test and indicating to the person that it's his ruin, then getting him to agree that the item, whatever it is, is a problem in his life.

No matter what the ruin, the prescription is the same—the Communication Course. Through that course, the person is told he will learn to communicate better, become happier, more confident, more responsible, and more "able." Communication, the universal solvent, contains the key for overcoming any problem in life. It's not unusual, the Registrar confides, for people who take the course to double or even triple their income.

Promises are made. Anything is said or done to convince the person to sign up for the Communication

Course. There's a reason for such pressure. As the Registrar knows, once the person begins that seemingly innocuous introductory course, he will be well on his way to becoming a Scientologist.

The cost of the course is nominal in comparison to other Scientology courses. It might run $50-$100. The length of the course is approximately two weeks, depending on frequency of attendance. What the new person doesn't know is that the introductory course is booby-trapped. It's a literal mind control minefield. It's designed to convert newcomers to Scientology so smoothly, they aren't even aware of the process.

How does it work?

Let's take an imaginary person named Mary. Mary stopped by the local Scientology center after a friend at work told her what a difference Scientology made in her marriage. She gave Mary a copy of the Dianetics book, which Mary did her best to read, though she found Hubbard's rambling writing style somewhat difficult to understand.

Mary sat through a lecture on Scientology that left her even more confused. The lecturer said that Scientology can be used to "handle" any problem in life, but how, Mary wonders, does it work?

After the lecture, Mary is introduced to the Registrar. During a long, friendly interview, in which Mary is asked about areas in her life in which she would like to see improvement, she discloses that she and her husband have been having marital problems.

The Registrar suddenly has the vital key—Mary's ruin. That's the one area in Mary's life she'd pay almost anything to see improved, or "handled."

"What you need," the Registrar assures her, "is the Communication Course. This is what will help your marriage. In that course, you'll learn vital communication techniques that you can use to improve your relationship with your husband.

"Don't you agree," he asks, "that by improving your communication skills, you would be able to improve the quality of your marriage?"

"Yes, I suppose so," Mary replies tentatively.

The Registrar, having been trained and drilled in hard-sell sales techniques, moves toward the "close." He gives examples of other people whose marriages were improved by taking the course. He may even call someone over to his desk to "double-team" with him and close Mary for the course.

"What have you got to lose?" he asks reasonably. "If, at the end of the course, you're not one hundred percent satisfied that the course has helped you, we'll give you your money back." He smiles and hands her a pen and enrollment form.

She signs.

"Wonderful," he says. "You're going to love the course. I can't wait to hear about your 'wins.'"

It's not that different from buying a used car. Scientology is probably the only church in the world in which the first meaningful transactions are with the Registrar and Cashier.

Mary is immediately given a "Routing Form" and a list of "terminals" or people she must see to get started on the course. One of the first of those is the Cashier. Mary will also be interviewed by the "Ethics Officer," the "Director of Processing," and various others, all of whom assure her that she just made one of the best decisions of her life.

Finally, Mary arrives in the course room where she is introduced to the "Course Supervisor," who, in many cases, will be wearing a military-like uniform, similar to a naval one, with shoulder epaulets, gold braid trim, and a lanyard around the neck.

The Supervisor hands her a "course pack," a bound collection of "bulletins," printed articles Hubbard wrote to be read during the course. At the beginning of the course pack is a check sheet, listing every item to be completed on the course, with a space for the student to initial each one. Each completed item is assigned a certain number of points.

Mary is given a seat in the course room. Feeling slightly disoriented and overwhelmed, she looks through the course pack. The first few bulletins are of an introductory nature, welcoming the student to Scientology. They're printed in different ink colors. Some are red, some green, some black. There seems to be a system to it, but Mary can't tell what it is.

She looks around the course room. It's different from any class she ever took before. She sits at a table with several other students. There's no talking except for one student who's checking out another on a bulletin. Everyone else studies silently.

There's no teacher, either. The Course Supervisor walks quietly around the room, taking notes on a clipboard, occasionally stopping to watch a particular student or hand a "pink sheet" to someone needing correction. The room has an almost military air. No talking is allowed except for check-outs.

In one of the first bulletins, Mary reads a set of rules for students on the course, entitled *Students' Guide to Acceptable Behavior.* All students must be on time for the course. Breaks will be strictly observed. No drugs or alcohol may be consumed within twenty-four hours of the course. Students aren't allowed to discuss their "case," or problems, with each other, and they aren't allowed to "evaluate" for or "invalidate" each other.

On one wall, a large, smiling picture of Hubbard looks out over the room. A life-sized bronze bust of Hubbard sits near the entrance.

In the back of the room, Mary observes students sitting in pairs, facing each other and staring silently into each other's eyes. Another pair of students stare at each other in the same way, but one is saying obscene things to the other. Mary feels uncomfortable about that, but she doesn't want to say anything, because she's new here, and, though some aspects of the class seem strange, she wants to make an effort to understand what's happening. Besides, the odd conversation doesn't seem to bother anyone else.

Like many people, Mary has a tendency to devalue her own perceptions and feelings in favor of the perceptions and feelings of others. She doesn't want to cause trouble or make a scene.

At 10:30 PM (the example is an evening course), the Supervisor says loudly, "That's it. End of course. Gather your materials and prepare for an after-class muster."

There's a flurry of noise and activity, as books are closed, and students in the back of the room pull their chairs up to the tables in the center.

Mary is given a piece of graph paper and is shown how to graph her "stats," or statistics, for the night. She adds up the points of all the items she completed on the check sheet and marks her total on the graph.

Then the Supervisor asks the students to share their "wins." Various students volunteer to give testimonies about what they learned during the course that evening.

The Supervisor announces they have a new student on the course and introduces Mary. She blushes as the others applaud. She has never been applauded for anything before.

"Mary, will you share your wins with us for this evening?" the Supervisor asks.

"Well, it's all very new to me. I hope I'll learn a lot here. It just seems different at first. Everyone has been very friendly, and I look forward to learning what this is all about."

People applaud again. The student on Mary's right places his hand on her shoulder and says, "Welcome," smiling and looking directly into her eyes.

On the way out of the building, several students stop Mary and tell her how glad they are that she is on the course.

"You'll really like it," they assure her. "This stuff really works. You'll see."

In the car on the way home, Mary feels the first stirring of hope, as she thinks about her husband. Maybe the class will help after all. Certainly, nothing else has.

As she thinks back over the events of the evening, one item sticks in her mind—everyone in Scientology seems friendly and genuinely happy. Maybe there's something to Scientology after all.

Mary just took her first step toward becoming a Scientologist.

As a newcomer to Scientology begins the Communication Course, he or she learns that, in addition to the bulletins, the course consists of a series of drills, called "training routines," designed to train someone to "communicate better."

What the person doesn't know—or suspect—is that the drills are actually a sophisticated set of mind-control processes designed to convert a newcomer into a confirmed Scientologist.

In the first training routine, called "TR-0," for Training Routine Zero, two students sit in chairs facing each other, knees almost touching, and stare into each other's eyes without blinking for a prolonged period of time. If either one blinks, moves, twitches, or has tears form in his eyes, he or she is flunked and told to start over.

During TR-0, a student may hallucinate and will almost certainly experience some sort of dissociation. However, the drill continues until the student can effortlessly maintain an unblinking stare with his partner.

In the second training routine, called TR-0 "bullbaited," the students follow the procedure of TR-0, but one must "bullbait" the other and "flatten his buttons." The student is allowed to do or say anything at all to make the other react, then flunk the person for reacting. That drill continues until each student can confront anything the partner says or does without reacting.

In doing TR-0 "bullbaited," students commonly use explicitly sexual material to provoke a reaction. That can include touching the other student. Verbal abuse is also condoned in the drill, with the justification that such abuse occurs in life and in "auditing," so the student must be prepared to "handle" it.

Suddenly, a hidden agenda has appeared on the course. It's surprising that so few students recognize it when it comes up.

The person entering Scientology has been sold the Communication Course to solve problems in his life. However, the wording in the instructions for the TRs, or training routines, suddenly refers to the fact that the new student is doing those drills to become more effective as an "auditor," the Scientology name for a counselor.

For example, in the instructions for TR-0, Hubbard wrote:

> To train student to
> confront a preclear (someone not
> yet Clear) with auditing only or
> with nothing.

In other words, the student comes to accept the fact that one reason for the course is to train him to become an "auditor." It's amazing that students on the course accept that subtle transition without question.

One analyst of the Communication Course, Ford Schwartz, wryly observed in an unpublished paper that the certificate for completing the Communication Course doesn't even mention the word *communication.* The certificate for completing the course certifies the student as a "Hubbard Apprentice Scientologist," or "HAS." Whether he likes it or not, upon completing the Communication Course, the new student has become a Scientologist!

In TR-1, the student is taught to give a command "newly and in a new unit of time," by choosing phrases from *Alice in Wonderland* and reading them to another student. Phrases such as the following are used in that drill.

"Would you please tell me why you're painting those roses?"

"Oh, please mind what you're doing!"

"Off with her head!"

"Curiouser and curiouser!"

"You shouldn't make jokes if it makes you so unhappy."

"Call the next witness!"

"Oh, you wicked, wicked little thing."

"Oh, you can't help that. We're all mad here."

In TR-2, a student is trained to control the communication of another person by the use of acknowledgements. For each phrase read to him from *Alice,* he responds with a firm, "Thank you!" or, "All right!" or, "I got that!"

In the third and fourth drills, a person is trained to get an answer to a question asked despite all efforts of the other person to distract him. The questions used in these drills are, "Do fish swim?" and, "Do birds fly?"

The drill isn't passed until the person performing the drill receives a satisfactory answer to the question. By the time that drill is passed, the student has learned to manipulate the communication of another person.

On one of the four "advanced TRs," the student learns to control the movements of another by shouting commands at him, such as, "Walk over to that wall!"

When the person does it, the student shouts, "Thank you!"

"Touch that wall! Thank you!"

"Walk over to that chair! Thank you!"

"Touch that chair! Thank you!"

When the student has learned to control another person, he learns to control objects, too. He is seated, facing a chair with an ashtray on it, and he must shout commands at the ashtray with such intensity that the ashtray rises off the chair on its own. Of course, that never happens, but that doesn't deter a Scientologist from trying.

The commands used on the ashtray are:

"Stand up!"

The person doing the drill raises the ashtray with his hand.

"Thank you! Sit down on that chair!"

He lowers the ashtray to the chair.

"Thank you!"

"Stand up! Thank you!"

What do such drills have to do with communication? Perhaps not as much as they have to do with the subject of control—specifically, learning to control and be controlled by others.

In her book, *Cults in America,* Willa Appel outlines three stages in any thought reform conversion process. First, the person is isolated physically and symbolically, from his past. Second, he's stripped of his identity through the mechanisms of humiliation and guilt. Third, he is converted to a new identity and worldview, that of the cult.[72]

That process is clearly evident in the Communication Course in Scientology, and that process isn't there by accident. It was placed there through careful design.

The process of isolation from the past is subtle and overt. The propaganda of Scientology overtly degrades many of the institutions in which the recruit previously placed his trust—family, friends, the government, educational institutions, and the established healing professions, to name a few.

Some of the ways in which the process of devaluation takes place are subtler. For example, the use of the term "wog," a derogatory term used in Scientology to refer to all non-Scientologists. Through the use of that word, the new Scientologist soon comes to understand that he, by virtue of being in Scientology, is superior to anyone not in Scientology.

Another technique used to separate the individual from his past is the renaming of everyday objects and experiences to new names unique to Scientology, understood only by other Scientologists.

For example, "reality" becomes "agreement." "Love" is renamed "ARC." The marital relationship is called the "second dynamic," while the "soul" becomes the "thetan." An argument becomes an "ARC break." A problem

---

[72] Appel, p. 77

becomes a "PTP." A secret becomes a "withhold." Even God is renamed to the "eighth dynamic."

Before he's been in Scientology for long, the initiate becomes versed in a language understood only inside the cult, creating a barrier between himself and friends or family outside the cult. As he increasingly adopts cult jargon, he can be understood only by other cult members.

For example, if a new Scientologist approached his college professor and told him that the reason he didn't have his homework finished was because he had a "PTP because of a missed withhold on the second dynamic," the chances are good that the professor would just stare blankly, yet every Scientologist would know what was meant.

The second stage of cult conversion is the stripping away of the old identity. Scientology accomplishes that in many ways.

The depersonalization of the individual in Scientology begins the moment he first walks though the front door. From the beginning, he learns to doubt and disregard his own perceptions.

What kind of church offers free personality tests to lure people in the front door? Why are hard-sell sales techniques used to market a class in communication? Why are the church members in uniform? Why are there so many odd, new words? Why are people doing such bizarre drills? What's really going on?

Instead of being allowed to question, the person is led to believe that all those things are part of the status quo of the "church" and are to be accepted without question.

Even during the initial sales presentation, the person's normal thinking process is bypassed. He's pressured into taking a course he knows little about, except for the Registrar's glowing promises.

In his book, *Deprogramming for Do-It-Yourselfers,* RK Heller points out that *highly orchestrated sales presentations may have the same effect as chanting; a person cannot hear his own thoughts. Questioning is postponed; then the question, forgotten.*[73]

The result of the sales presentation in Scientology is that the person becomes convinced that he has a problem, and that Scientology provides the only answer to it. Before he reaches the classroom, the student is subjected to a "routing form," in which he must submit to be interviewed by several authority figures in the organization before being allowed "on course"—the gauntlet approach to education.

Once on the course, the person suddenly finds himself in a quasi-military situation, again within a "church," and that seems accepted by everyone as normal. Because of social conditioning, he avoids asking an obvious or embarrassing question for fear of social rejection. That same social conditioning, the desire to please others and not question, together with carefully planned group reinforcement, provide incentive for the newcomer to gradually surrender his old identity and accept the new one of Scientologist.

When the new student is introduced, he or she is greeted with applause, decreasing the odds that he might raise any objections while on course.

In studying the Scientology materials, the new student quickly learns that to question any of Hubbard's writings is expressly forbidden. Any disagreement with the contents of the course materials is considered a misunderstanding on the student's part. He's advised to "look up his misunderstood word," to see what it was he hasn't properly understood. Doubting the materials isn't permitted, as "doubt" is a "lower condition," punishable within Scientology.

---

[73] Heller, p. 91

A student in Scientology is forbidden to ask questions, think, or doubt.

The new person in Scientology is "love bombed," which means being given much attention and approbation for being there. The honeymoon, however, is short-lived. The new Scientologist soon learns that continued love and acceptance is conditional upon giving time or money to the organization on a continuing basis.

A student isn't considered a "completion" on the Communication Course until he's ready and eager to sign up for the next course in Scientology. The true result of the Communication Course is that the person has become a Scientologist, and it says so on his certificate. He is also motivated to continue further indoctrination in Scientology in the form of his "next course."

The conclusion, according to Ford Schwartz, is that the Communication Course in Scientology is a *manipulative, systematic process, an integral part of which is the conversion of new members. It is the subtlety with which the transformation takes place which makes it a threat to unsuspecting people.*

As Schwartz describes, the new member is being subjected to a hidden agenda of which he is totally unaware:

- The person has come into Scientology with a normal life problem and is induced to take a course in communication that will help him with that problem.
- He's subjected to a hard-sell approach that plays upon his vulnerability. He's made a number of promises concerning the course and what it will do in his life.
- In his dealings with the church, he's immediately and thereafter placed in an inferior position and is thereby more susceptible to manipulation and control.

- He's subjected to high-stress drills that can produce dissociative states and hallucinations.
- His past educational experience and accomplishments are negated.
- Key words in his native language are redefined, creating shifts in understanding and manipulation of thought to conform to the cult's paradigm.
- The hidden agenda of becoming a Scientologist is subtly introduced during the Communication Course.

Slowly and subconsciously, the student comes to identify himself with the group and with his new identity of being a Scientologist.

The student is no longer free to think, question, or doubt.

What's remarkable is the smoothness with which the transition to the new paradigm of Scientology is made by most people who take the course. Social conditioning, learned behavior assimilated throughout life, becomes a liability in dealing with the sinister manipulation of a cult like Scientology. The student unthinkingly walks into the trap.

In the greatest redefinition of all, the new Scientologist, believing himself to be on the "Road to Total Freedom," is instead on the road to becoming a willing slave.

CHAPTER FIVE

Dianetics—May You Never Be the Same Again

The creation of Dianetics is a milestone for Man comparable to his discovery of fire and superior to his inventions of the wheel and arch....

This is useful knowledge. With it the blind again see, the lame walk, the ill recover, the insane become sane, and the sane become saner.

L. Ron Hubbard

Who are you? Have you lived before? What is your name? Say your name over to yourself a few times. Say it over and over. Come on, say it some more. Now say your name a few more times. Now say it a few more just to make sure of it.

That is right. Better go back and do it a few more times if you missed.

All right. Now let's ask it again. Who are you? Where did you really come from? How do you know you haven't lived before?

Dianetics techniques

> indicate that you have. And
> Dianetics, which has revealed so
> much to the Western World,
> comes up now with this strange
> data. You are you. But you may
> have lived elsewhere under
> another name without even
> suspecting it yourself.
>
> L. Ron Hubbard, *Have You
> Lived Before This Life?*

The book *Dianetics: The Modern Science of Mental Health* is to Scientologists much the same as the Bible is to Christians: the indisputable word of God (Hubbard) that provides the rationale for belief and the basis for faith.

Interestingly, just as there are many Christians who don't read the Bible, there are many Scientologists who either haven't read *Dianetics* or who have tried and been put off by its style, which one writer called, *abstruse, rambling, repetitive, studded with confusion, neologism, and littered with interminable footnotes.*[74]

Despite its style, however, the Dianetics book was a publisher's dream. Although the original printing was a cautious 6,000 copies, and initial sales were slow, by the end of 1950, sales reached over 150,000 copies. The book sparked an avalanche of interest across the country in its new, do-it-yourself psychotherapy.

Part of the book's success had to do with the sweeping promises Hubbard made throughout the book. Never one to be modest, he claimed that in Dianetics, *the hidden source of all psychosomatic ills and human aberration has been discovered, and skills have been developed for their invariable cure.*

---

[74] Miller, p. 155

He grandiloquently surveys the scope of Dianetics in the beginning of the book:

> A science of mind is a goal
> which has engrossed thousands
> of generations of man. Armies,
> dynasties, and whole civilizations
> have perished for the lack of it.
> Rome went to dust for the want
> of it. And down in the arsenal is
> an atom bomb, its hopeful nose
> full-armed in ignorance of it.
>
> No quest has been more
> relentlessly pursued or has been
> more violent. No primitive tribe,
> no matter how ignorant, has
> failed to recognize the problem as
> a problem, nor has it failed to
> bring forth at least an attempted
> formulation.

In Dianetics, he concluded, the answer had finally been found.

His promises of salvation were like manna from heaven for the thousands of souls who sought then, and still seek, relief from the vicissitudes of life. Like shipwreck survivors in a tossing sea, people by the thousands grasped desperately for the lifeline Hubbard dangled from the passing rescue ship. The recently formed Hubbard Dianetic Research Foundation in Elizabeth, New Jersey, was inundated with calls and letters requesting more information about the new "science."

The problem, according to Hubbard, was basically simple. The mind was like a computer. In the *Evolution of a Science,* a small book he wrote telling the story of his discovery of Dianetics, he wrote:

> The optimum brain should
> be able to recall any perception,

> even the trivial, asleep and
> awake from the beginning of life
> to death. It should think with
> such swiftness that vocal
> pondering would be unutterably
> unable to keep pace with a
> thousandth part of one
> computation. And...it should
> never be wrong.[75]

The mind, which in Dianetics theory is composed of what are called "memory banks," *contains a complete color-visio record of a person's whole life. Every perception observed in a lifetime is to be found in the [memory] banks. All the perceptions. In good order.*[76]

The memories, he continues, are filed by time. They have an age and an emotional label, a state of physical being label, and a precise and exhaustive record of everything perceived by organic sensation, smell, taste, tactile, audio, and visio perceptics plus the train of thought of the analyzer of that moment.[77]

Something must be wrong. Most of us can't remember every memory, awake or asleep, of our lives. Why not?

There is, Hubbard explains, a villain in the piece, known in Dianetics as the "reactive mind." The reactive mind is the dark side of the mind, similar in function to the subconscious mind of psychoanalysis.

> The reactive mind thinks in
> identities. It is a stimulus-
> response mind. Its actions are
> exteriorly determined. It has no

---

[75] Hubbard, *Evolution of a Science*, p. 11

[76] Ibid, p. 57

[77] Ibid, p. 57

power of choice. It puts physical
pain data forward in an effort to
save the organism. So long as its
mandates and commands are
obeyed it withholds the physical
pain. As soon as the organism
starts to go against its
commands, it inflicts the pain.[78]

The contents of the reactive mind are "engrams," and other memories that function as reminders of the engrams are called "locks."

An engram is an energy
picture. It is made during a
period of physical pain when the
analyzer is out of circuit and the
organism experiences something
it conceives to be or which is
contrary to survival. An engram
is received only in the absence of
the analytical power.[79]

The engram contains the memory of actual physical pain and unconsciousness, known in Dianetics as "anaten."

For example, suppose Johnny is playing with his sister, Susie, in the kitchen, while Mommy's doing the laundry. It's raining outside. There is the sound of running water and the smell of bleach on the air.

Susie hits Johnny on the right side of the head with a toy, hard enough to cut the skin and momentarily knock him unconscious. The elements of an engram are present—pain and unconsciousness. The memory of the

---

[78] Ibid, p. 66

[79] Ibid, p. 67

experience would be filed in Johnny's reactive mind as an engram.

Years later, the adult Johnny finds that every time it rains, he tends to get a headache, and it's always on the right side of his head. His mysterious headaches also occur whenever his wife does the laundry, and he hears water running or smells bleach. Experiences that are similar in content to an original engram produce the same physical responses as in the engram being "restimulated."

Through Dianetic auditing, Hubbard promised that Johnny could be taken back in time through earlier and earlier memories of headaches to the original engram that holds the chain of memories in place in the mind. Once Johnny recalls the original memory of the time when Susie hit him in the head, the engram is discharged and can no longer produce reactive effects in the present.

In that way, Hubbard promised that freedom from all psychosomatic problems could be achieved through Dianetic auditing. The person who, through auditing, discharged all the engrams from his reactive mind would achieve the state of Clear, in which he no longer has a reactive mind. Its contents have been refiled in the analytical mind and are available for conscious recall by the Clear.

> Refile the reactive
> memories and the whole
> conscious lifetime of the
> individual springs into view,
> brilliant and clear, unmodified by
> the bypass circuits which are
> madness. Reduce the reactive
> mind and the optimum mind for
> the individual comes into view.[80]

---

[80] Ibid, p. 75

If Dianetics had sprung full-blown from Hubbard's mind, and if, in practice, it yielded the stellar results promised for it, then Hubbard might've achieved legitimate fame.

The fact is that in Dianetics, Hubbard's genius was more for synthesis than thesis. While in the Oak Knoll Naval Hospital in 1945, Hubbard spent hours in the medical library, doing research that would find fruition in the publication of *Dianetics* five years later.

One man who researched Hubbard's researches, Jeff Jacobsen, said that in creating Dianetics, Hubbard may have drawn from the works of at least seven well-known researchers in the field of the mind, some of whose writings were published just prior to Hubbard's stay in Oak Knoll. That writer stated that Hubbard drew from the work of two men, Drs. Sadger and Pailthorpe, who published in the *Psychoanalytic Review* in 1941, and who stressed the importance of prenatal memories in mental pathology.[81]

Other sources for Dianetics cited by Jacobsen include Freud's abreaction therapy, in which early memories are relived, thereby discharging their power in later life; Korzybski's General Semantics, in which a concept very similar to the reactive mind is explored; the book *The Mneme,* by Simon, where the word *engram* was originally coined; and the science of Cybernetics, which was very popular at the time Hubbard wrote *Dianetics.*

Hubbard always claimed that a great deal of research and testing went into Dianetics:

> The discoveries and
> developments which made the
> formulation of Dianetics possible
> occupied many years of exact

---

[81] Jacobsen, p. 1-3

research and careful testing.[82]

Discovered, computed, and organized by L. Ron Hubbard, mathematician and theoretical philosopher, DIANETICS has been under study for twenty-five years and in active formulation for the past eleven.[83]

By early 1950, over two hundred patients had been tested; of those two hundred people, two hundred cures had been obtained. Dianetics is a science, because by following readily prescribed techniques, which can be specifically stated, based on definitely stated basic postulates, a specifically described result can be obtained in every case.[84]

Hubbard applied the first step of the scientific method: he stated his hypothesis. Unfortunately, he ignored the remaining steps of the scientific process. It was his promise of scientific testing that drew some of the early professionals into Hubbard's early circle.

Hubbard's failure to produce even a single empirical test for Dianetics was also the reason why many of those same professionals left Hubbard almost as quickly as they arrived.

Jacobsen states, "Anyone can make as many outlandish claims as he wants, but the research must be

---

[82] Hubbard, *Dianetics: Modern Science of Mental Health,* p. 1

[83] Hubbard, from the original *Dianetics* book jacket

[84] Hubbard, *Evolution of a Science,* p. 95

accessible and reproducible to support those claims if he brandishes scientific validity."[85]

Dianetics, and Scientology for that matter, have yet to be subjected to empirical validation by the scientific method. Until they are, these "mental sciences" remain just another brand of snake oil.

As the practice of Dianetics evolved during the early 1950s, Hubbard began introducing the concept of past lives into auditing with increasing frequency, another clue to his relationship with his mentor, Aleister Crowley, in whose occult circle the pursuit of past-life memories was a frequent diversion.

The addition of the belief in reincarnation surfaced publicly in Scientology in 1958, in another strange Hubbard book, *Have You Lived Before This Life?* In the introduction, Hubbard wrote:

> In the past the term
> reincarnation has mystified man.
> The definition has been
> corrupted. The word has been
> taken to mean to be born again
> in different life forms, whereas its
> actual definition is to be born
> again into the flesh or into
> another body. In order that there
> can be rebirth, something must
> enter in. This is the being, the
> person himself. It is YOU.

> The existence of past lives
> is proven in Scientology.

> The concept of
> reincarnation and Man's belief in
> the past and future continuum is
> as old as Man himself. It can be

[85] Jacobsen, p. 4

traced to the beginnings of thirty-one primitive cultures and has dominated almost every religion through history as a pivotal belief.

The Egyptians, Hindus, Buddhists, Jainists, Sikhists, Brahmans, Neo Platonists, Christians, Romans, Jews, and Gnostics all believed in reincarnation and the rebirth cycle.

It was a fundamental belief in the Roman Catholic Church until 553 AD, when a company of four monks held the Synod of Constantinople (without the pope present) and decided the belief could not exist. They condemned the teaching of reincarnation as heresy, and it was at this time that references to it were expunged from the Bible.

Without reference to the subject as the written word, the belief fell to the mystics and spiritualists of the middle ages. These, too, were defeated, but the belief persisted and again was rediscovered in the 19th century in the beginnings of psychology.

Freud and Jung acknowledged Man's belief in his own immortality and reincarnation. Their mistake was only in assigning this basic truth to imagination or fantasy.

Today in Scientology, the

stigma of the subject has been erased and verification of the existence of past lives is fact.

To some, these facts may come as a surprise. To others, it may be as casual as looking at an old photo album. But to everyone it will be a unique and enlightening adventure into the past, all in the course of discovering a brighter future.[86]

The "remembering" of past lives in Dianetics has become tradition. In Dianetic auditing, the student is coaxed to remember earlier and earlier experiences. He will know from other students that memory of past lives is expected. The expectation is enforced by a process called "Review auditing," in which the student who is reluctant or unable to "remember his past lives" is given special "remedies" to handle that obstacle. The fact that the Review auditing is even more expensive than regular auditing—at several hundred dollars an hour—provides incentive for the student to overcome his inability to "remember" as quickly as possible.

In Dianetic auditing, procedure is followed strictly by the book. A set of rote commands is used in this auditing, and they must be delivered exactly as written. The "items" to be "run" are various physical or psychosomatic problems that are located in an assessment done on the E-meter before the Dianetic auditing is begun.

Examples of "somatics" that can be run in Dianetics are: a sharp pain in the forehead, pain in the stomach, a burning sensation in the eyes, feeling hot, an itching sensation on the skin, or a feeling of fear, sadness, anger, etc.

---

[86] Hubbard, *Have You Lived Before This Life?* p. 1

The commands used in Dianetics go something like this:

"Locate an incident containing 'a sharp pain in the forehead.'"

"When was it?"

"What is the duration of the incident?"

"Move to the beginning of the incident and tell me when you are there."

"What do you see?"

"Scan through to the end of the incident."

"Tell me what happened."

"Is there an earlier incident containing 'a sharp pain in the forehead?'"

An interesting example of "running past lives" is given in Hubbard's book, *Have You Lived Before This Life?* and is reproduced here. The dialogue alternates between the Preclear (the person being audited), and the Auditor.

Auditor: Are you interested in running "pain in the left side?"

Preclear: Yes.

Auditor: OK. Locate an incident of another causing you "pain in the left side."

Preclear: Yes. Got one.

Auditor: Good. When was it?

Preclear: It was my accident two months ago.

Auditor: Good. Move to that incident.

Preclear: OK.

Auditor: What is the duration of the incident.

Preclear: Well, less than a minute.

Auditor: OK. Move to the beginning of the incident.

Preclear: Uh-huh. (Eyes closed)

Auditor: What do you see?

Preclear: A street and the inside of my car.

Auditor: All right. Move through the incident to a point "less than a minute" later.

Preclear: (Preclear does this and then opens his eyes.)

Auditor: Tell me what happened.

Preclear: I started up when the light turned green, then suddenly, I heard brakes, and it was like a big bump—but really hard—as the other car crashed into the side of my car. I smacked into the car door just as it buckled, then my car slid off to the right and came to a stop against a street lamp.

Auditor: OK. Move to the beginning of the incident. Tell me when you are there.

Preclear: All right.

OK. Scan through to the end of the incident.

Preclear: (Silent) OK.

Auditor: Tell me what happened.

Preclear: I was starting into the intersection, and I heard the screech of brakes. And then a smash as his car plowed into mine. The car door buckled just as I slammed against it. Then my car skipped to the right and into a streetlamp post. I was startled. I felt my side, and it was all bloody. Then it started to hurt. I held my hand there to stop the bleeding. I thought I'd die.

Auditor: All right. Is there an earlier incident of another causing you "pain in the left side?"

Preclear: Yes, there is.

Auditor: Good. When was it?

Preclear: 1962—spring.

Auditor: All right. Move to that incident.

Preclear: Uh-huh.

Auditor: What is the duration of the incident?

Preclear: About a week.

Auditor: OK. Move to the beginning of the incident.

Preclear: OK. (Eyes closed)

Auditor: What do you see?

Preclear: The football field and stadium at my high

school.

Auditor: All right. Move through the incident to a point "about a week" later.

Preclear: (Silently does this, then looks up)

Auditor: Tell me what happened.

Preclear: I went out for the track team and after school, we jogged around and around the field—to get into shape. I got an excruciating pain in my side almost every day for two weeks.

Auditor: OK. Move to the beginning of the incident. Tell me when you are there.

Preclear: I'm there.

Auditor: Good. Scan through to the end of the incident.

Preclear: (Silently does this) OK.

Auditor: Tell me what happened.

Preclear: We ran around and around the field, and the coach pushed us a little harder each day, and each day, the pain would turn on in my side. It hurt terribly.

Auditor: All right. Is there an earlier incident of another causing you "pain in the left side?"

Preclear: Ummm.... (long pause) Yes, I guess so.

Auditor: Good. When was it?

Preclear: World War One, I think. It was 1917.

Auditor: All right. Move to that incident.

Preclear: OK. I did it.

Auditor: Good. What is the duration of the incident?

Preclear: Two or three minutes—it's pretty short.

Auditor: OK. Move to the beginning of the incident.

Preclear: OK. (Eyes closed)

Auditor: Fine. What do you see?

Preclear: Well, I can see no-man's land in the flashes of explosions and a soldier coming at me with a bayonet.

Auditor: Good. Move through the incident to a point "two or three minutes" later.

Preclear: (Silent, then opens his eyes)

Auditor: What happened?

Preclear: I was up over the embankment out in front of the trenches, and suddenly, I saw a soldier coming at me with a bayonet. He stabbed me in the side with it.

Auditor: All right. Move to the beginning of the incident. Tell me when you are there.

Preclear: Uh-huh.

Auditor: Scan through to the end of the incident.

Preclear: (Does so silently) Uh-huh.

Auditor: Tell me what happened.

Preclear: I was out in front of the trenches—we were running forward. There were cannons firing, and there were flashes from explosions now and then. I suddenly saw an enemy soldier. I called out to warn the men I was with. The soldier leaped at me with his bayonet and stabbed me in the side. It hurt a lot, and I bled a lot. I was taken back to a field hospital behind the lines, where I died a few days later.

Auditor: All right. Is there an earlier incident of another causing you "pain in the left side?"

Preclear: Let me see.... Yes, there is.

Auditor: Good. When was it?

Preclear: Oh, it had to be...it was 1823.

Auditor: All right. Move to that incident.

Preclear: OK.

Auditor: Good. What is the duration of the incident?

Preclear: Five minutes.

Auditor: All right. Move to the beginning of the incident.

Preclear: All right. (Eyes closed)

Auditor: What do you see?

Preclear: A gatehouse, two horses, trees, a road.

Auditor: OK. Move through the incident to a point "five minutes" later.

Preclear: (Silent, then opens eyes)

Auditor: What happened?

Preclear: I had ridden up the road toward a big estate. I'd stopped at the gatehouse and was just getting back onto my horse when he shied and threw me against another rider beside me. I hurt my side against his boot and stirrup. It was very painful, and I had to be helped back onto my horse, and I rode slowly on up the road.

Auditor: All right. Move to the beginning of the incident. Tell me when you are there.

Preclear: Yes.

Auditor: Scan through to the end of the incident.

Preclear: (Silent) OK.

Auditor: Tell me what happened.

Preclear: I had been riding fast to give my neighbor some news—I was very upset—I don't know what about, though it seems like someone had died or was dying. I stopped to tell the gateman what had happened. I ran out to get on my horse, and, as I was mounting, the horse shied and threw me to the left. I landed against the boot and stirrup of a rider next to me, then fell to the ground. It knocked the wind out of me and hurt like the dickens. I was helped up onto my horse.

(Preclear laughs) Well, that's a relief. I mean, the pain's gone. That's all there was to it. I scared my horse. Oh! And that's why I hurt so much when I was running in school—it was like riding the horse that day—pushing him faster and faster. And then the pain would start. It was the same pain. No wonder. Well, that's the end of that. (Preclear grinning)[87]

A successful Dianetics session always ends with a "cognition" on the part of the Preclear, as well as what are called in Dianetics "very good indicators," meaning that the Preclear is smiling and looking good.

In Hubbard's writings about Dianetics, he claims to be able to cure almost every illness imaginable. For example:

> Psychosomatic ills, such as
> arthritis, migraine, ulcers,

---

[87] Ibid, p. 19

allergies, asthma, coronary
difficulties (psychosomatic—
about one-third of all heart
trouble cases), tendonitis,
bursitis, paralysis (hysterical),
eye trouble (nonpathological),
have all responded as intended
by the therapist, without failure
in any case.

(From the inner front flap
of the original Dianetics book
jacket)

The claims made for the Clear in the Dianetics are spectacular:

A clear can be tested for
any and all psychoses, neuroses,
compulsions, and repressions (all
aberrations) and can be
examined for any autogenic (self-
generated) diseases referred to as
psychosomatic ills. These tests
confirm the clear to be entirely
without such ills or aberrations.
Additional tests of his intelligence
indicate it to be high above the
current norm. Observation of his
activity demonstrates that he
pursues existence with vigor and
satisfaction.[88]

Hubbard harbored a special grudge against psychiatrists. In a policy letter on psychiatry, he stated:

A full psychoanalysis
covering five years cost a decade
ago 9,000 pounds (British

---

[88] Hubbard, *Dianetics: Modern Science of Mental Health*, p. 8

sterling). Yet we furnish far more lasting a result for $500.... It costs about $75,000 to educate a psychiatrist who can obtain no good result. For $500 or less, we can train a Hubbard Dianetic auditor who can run rings around any commie psychiatrist on the planet.... Any HAS (the lowest-level Scientologist) knows more and can do more about the mind than any psychiatrist.[89]

Hubbard claimed that Dianetics could cure leukemia:

Leukemia is evidently psychosomatic in origin and at least eight cases of leukemia have been treated successfully by Dianetics after medicine had traditionally given up. The source of leukemia has been reported to be an engram containing the phrase, "It turns my blood to water."[90]

In *A History of Man,* Hubbard claims the ability to cure the ultimate disease—cancer:

Mitosis is an incident. Cellular division, once or many times, is on common record. Mitosis answers the conditions for the other type of cancer—the malignant cell.

Cancer has been eradicated by auditing out

---

[89] Hubbard bulletin, *Psychiatry.*

[90] Hubbard bulletin of May, 1953, *The Old Man's Case Book*

conception and mitosis.[91]

The sad fact is that there have been many cases of people in Scientology seeking cures for cancer and other terminal conditions through Dianetic auditing, and, sadly, ignoring more traditional medical help that might have prolonged their lives.

Hubbard claimed many times to have the answer to every type of psychosis and neurosis, announcing at one time that these cases could be handled in between 8-35 hours of auditing.

Some of the most interesting Hubbard curiosa occur when he attempts to expound upon medical topics. One such example is outlined in a policy he wrote concerning arthritis:

> Arthritis, then, is
> structurally a deposit of calcium,
> or other mineral, in an area
> which has been restricted by an
> old injury. The injury is held in
> suspension and in place in the
> area by restimulation of the
> environment which contains
> some of the factors present when
> that area was injured. It is a
> condition of such an injury, in
> order to be in suspension
> sufficiently to cause arthritis,
> that the sufferer himself must
> have administered a like injury to
> another person.[92]

In another curious bulletin on eyesight and eyeglasses, Hubbard wrote:

---

[91] Hubbard, *A History of Man*, p. 20

[92] Hubbard bulletin of August, 1952, *The Handling of Arthritis*

> It is interesting to know
> that a thetan doesn't look
> through his eyeballs. He has two
> little gold discs, one in front of
> each eye lens. These are not the
> lenses of the eyes, but, as you
> might say, mocked-up energy.
> They are little gold discs that are
> superimposed over the eye, and
> he looks through these. The
> eyeballs merely serve to locate
> these discs.[93]

By auditing the person on these discs, Hubbard claimed to produce fantastic changes in eyesight. In the same bulletin, he explained astigmatism:

> Astigmatism, a distortion
> of image, is only an anxiety to
> alter the image. You get an
> astigmatic condition when a
> person is trying to work it over
> into a substitute, if he possibly
> can. Here again it is a case of not
> enough—he didn't have enough.

Is that clear?

Hubbard claimed that auditing could eliminate a person's vulnerability to radiation, and he claimed the Scientologists would, as a result, be the only ones to live through World War III. He first wrote:

> As cosmic rays, gamma, X-
> rays, et al, apparently move
> through solids without
> encountering resistance, they

---

[93] Hubbard, Professional Auditor's Bulletin no. 111, 1 May 1957,

Eyesight and Glasses

then invalidate solids. This is a direct invalidation of the solidity of anything including a mock-up. Thus it tends to say a thing is not there—thus that a creation has not been made....

Radiation, then, is the proof that a thing solid is not solid. This is an invalidation that one has created. Thus radiation is seen to hit at all creativeness. Its irresponsibility factor is also this—one cannot be responsible for things which are proven not to exist....

This also tells us that time began on an invalidation of solids....

In actual proof Procedure CHH [a Scientology auditing procedure] resolves radiation.[94]

One year later, he wrote:

I have been conducting a series of experiments, one of them almost fatal to myself, on the auditing of radiation burns. I have found that we can make an enormous affect upon radiation burns and can cure them in a milder form. That means we are the only agency, the only people on the face of the Earth, who can cure the effect of atomic

---

[94] Hubbard bulletin of 3 June 1957, *Explanation of Aberrative Character of Radiation*

> radiation. I expect to make
> further progress in this direction
> and the whole answer is not yet
> gained, for the whole answer
> would be to actually proof a body
> against radiation itself.[95]

Hubbard later "solved" this problem, claiming that a body could be "proofed against radiation" by taking megadoses of the vitamin niacin.

Hubbard's insights into the illnesses of human beings were also aided by his innovative work with plants. An example of that follows:

> Recently I have been
> studying life sources and
> reactions in plants. I have gained
> data now which, in preliminary
> look, indicates that a plant
> becomes ill only pursuant to a
> series of shocks which make "it
> decide" it cannot survive. Only
> after that does it "cooperate" with
> a disease. Up to that time it
> cannot seem to get ill....
>
> This bears itself out in
> human beings more obviously
> than in plants. Illness follows
> postulates to die.[96]

These are just a few examples of the writings of Hubbard re: the "science" of Dianetics, the "milestone for Man comparable to his discovery of fire and superior to his inventions of the wheel and the arch...."

---

[95] Hubbard, Professional Auditor's Bulletin no. 74, *The Atomic Fizzle*

[96] Hubbard, policy letter of 7 July 1959, *Staff Auditing Requirements*

Other than being an adventure in fantasy for those so inclined, is there any harm to Dianetics? Yes, say two researchers who have looked into Scientology in some depth. Flo Conway and Jim Siegelman believe that *prolonged auditing can cause people to experience "increasingly realistic hallucinations" so that eventually the individual can no longer "distinguish between what he is experiencing and what he is only imagining."*[97] This, indeed, is the true danger of Dianetics.

Hubbard poses a final question for his followers:

Up there are the stars.
Down in the arsenal is an atom bomb.

Which one is it going to be?[98]

The book *Dianetics: the Modern Science of Mental Health* can still be found on the shelves of most bookstores today, its yellow cover beckoning yet another person to pick it up and discover the *Road to Total Freedom.*

Could it be the road to nowhere?

---

[97] Rudin, p. 90

[98] Hubbard, *Evolution of a Science,* p. 105

CHAPTER SIX

Grade 0 to Clear—The Yellow Brick Road to Total Freedom

The E-meter is never wrong. It sees all. It knows all. It tells everything.

L. Ron Hubbard

A Clear can be tested for any and all psychoses, neuroses, compulsions, and repressions and can be examined for any autogenetic (self-generated) diseases referred to as psychosomatic ills. These tests confirm the Clear to be entirely without such ills or aberrations.

Dianetics: Modern Science of Mental Health, by L. Ron Hubbard

Hanging on the wall of every Scientology organization around the world is a large chart, lettered in red ink, and boldly labeled across the top, *The Bridge to Total Freedom.* The chart lists the main courses available in Scientology, arranged in hierarchical sequence.

In the instructions at the bottom of the chart, Hubbard wrote:

It is hard for Man in his present condition to even grasp

that higher states of being exist. He had no literature about them, really, or any vocabulary for them.

Factually, you've been traveling this universe a very long time without a map.

Now you've got one.

On the following page is a chart of the "processing levels" of Scientology. These are the levels through which a person will progress from first beginning in Scientology to achieving the celebrated state of Clear.

Processing Levels of Scientology

LevelAbilities	Gained
OT VIII	Confidential
OT VII	Confidential
OT VI	Confidential
OT V	Confidential
OT IV	Confidential
OT III	Confidential
OT II	Confidential
OT I	Confidential
Clear	A being who no longer has a reactive mind
Solo	Freedom from dramatization and return of powers to act on own determinism
Grade 4 (Abilities)	Moving out of fixed conditions and
gaining abilities to do new things	
Grade 3 (Upsets)	Freedom from the upsets of the past and ability to face the future
Grade 2 (Overts and Withholds)	Relief from the hostilities and sufferings of life
Grade 1 (Problems)	Ability to recognize the source of problems and make them vanish
Grade 0 (Communication)	Ability to communicate freely with anyone on any subject

Dianetics	A healthy, happy human being
ARC Straightwire	Knows he/she won't get any worse
Objectives	In present time and able to control and put order in the environment

The lowest level of auditing in Scientology consists of what are called the "objective processes." These are often programmed for a newcomer to Scientology after he has completed the introductory course. The stated purpose of these drills is "to get the preclear more in touch with his environment (reality)." The hypnotic content of the drills, however, could indicate that they were conceived to do just the opposite.

One of the most frequently used of the "objectives" is a process called "Opening Procedure by Duplication," or, more familiarly, "OP Pro by Dup." In that process, the preclear is taken into a room in which two objects are placed, usually on a table, several feet from each other, so the preclear must walk to get from one to the other.

The commands of the drill are:
"Go over to the book."
"Look at it."
"Pick it up."
"What is its color?"
"What is its temperature?"
"What is its weight?"
"Put it down in exactly the same place."
"Go over to the ashtray."
"Look at it."
"Pick it up."
"What is its color?"
"What is its temperature?'
"What is its weight?"
"Put it down in exactly the same place."
"Go over to the book." Etc.

The drill may be done for several hours at a time, "until the preclear can do it without delay, without protest, without apathy, but with cheerfulness."[99]

Other examples of Objective processes include the commands:

"Spot some spots in your body," alternating with, "Spot some spots in the room," and continued for at least an hour;

"Examine your chair," alternated with, "Examine the floor," and continued for at least an hour;

"Where's your face?" given continuously for at least an hour; and

"Start laughing," "Keep on laughing," "Laugh," and "Keep on laughing," given alternately for at least an hour.[100]

In another series of fifteen objective processes called the CCHs (abbreviations for the words Control, Communication, and Havingness, the last a Scientology word), a preclear is steered around the room for hours at a time with the commands:

"Look at that wall. Thank you."

"Walk over to that wall. Thank you."

"With the right hand, touch that wall. Thank you."

"Turn around. Thank you."[101]

---

[99] Hubbard, *Creation of Human Ability,* p. 47

[100] Ibid, p. 269

[101] Hubbard, bulletin on CCHs 1-15

In his book, *Creation of Human Ability,* Hubbard acknowledges that some people might think such drills hypnotic. In actuality, he states, the drills "run out" hypnosis. *(They) induce no trances. People who think so simply don't know much about hypnosis.*[102]

In ARC Straightwire, the second level on "the Bridge," the emphasis is upon improving a person's ability to recall memories from the past. ARC is an acronym for Affinity, Reality, and Communication, which together equate to "understanding" in Scientology. The commands on that fairly innocuous level are:

"Recall something that was really real to you."

"Recall a time when you were in good communication with someone."

"Recall a time when you really liked someone."

"Recall a time you knew you understood someone."[103]

Dianetics auditing was originally prescribed in Scientology after a person had completed some "objectives" and ARC Straightwire and before progressing onto the grades. Currently, Dianetics is administered after a person has completed the grades.

Each grade from 0-4 isolates and addresses a different area of common life problems. On each grade are hundreds of processes and commands, from which just a few examples will be given here.

On Grade Zero, the promised ability gained is an *ability to communicate freely to anyone on any subject.* The commands, "What are you willing to talk to me about?" and "What would you like to tell me about it?" are given

---

[102] Hubbard, *Creation of Human Ability,* p. 271

[103] Hubbard bulletin *0-IV Expanded Grade Processes – Triples—ARC Straightwire*

alternately and combined with other commands until the person has the promised revelation.

On Grade One, the focus is on problems, and the preclear is asked questions like, "What problem could you confront?" and "What problem would you rather not confront?" until the person comes to realize he *has the ability to recognize the source of problems and make them vanish.*

On Grade Two, the preclear is grilled on questions such as:

"Tell me some things you think you should not have done to another."

"Tell me what you've done to another that got you into trouble."

"What have you done to another that you regret?"

"What have you said to another that you wish you hadn't?"

This continues until he or she comes to realize that *I have attained relief from feelings of guilt or regret about past actions of mine, and do not feel I must keep secret anything that has happened.*

On Grade Three, which addresses areas of past upset in life and the person's ability to deal with change, the questions are, "What do you want changed?" and "What do you want unchanged?"

The person is finished with that level when he feels he has *discovered through auditing the source of past upsets,* and now understands and feels free of such upsets, and when he is able to face the future.

Grade Four deals with psychological strategies used by the person to make him right and others wrong. These are called *service facsimiles* in Scientology. The questions on that level are:

"In this lifetime, what do you use to make others wrong?"

Then, for each answer given to that question, the following are asked:

"In this lifetime, how would _____ make you right?"

"In this lifetime, how would _____ make others wrong?"

"In this lifetime, how would _____ help you escape domination?"

"In this lifetime, how would _____ help you dominate others?"

"In this lifetime, how would _____ aid your survival?"

"In this lifetime, how would _____ hinder the survival of others?"

When the person attests that he's been *released from fixed and destructive patterns of action and now feels free to do new things,* he can move to more advanced processing on the road to the state of Clear and above.

All levels above Grade Four are considered confidential within Scientology. The materials are carried about in locked briefcases chained to the preclear's arm with a dog leash. There's a great aura of secrecy and importance about those levels and the people who are on them.

On all lower levels in Scientology, the preclear is audited by another person, but, on the secret upper levels, he must audit himself, a skill acquired in the Solo Course, which is a preparatory course for all upper levels.

On the Solo Course, Hubbard discloses the inner structure of the reactive mind. The core of the reactive mind, he explains, is called the *R6 bank.* Surrounding it are the various engrams and locks that have been removed by earlier Dianetic and Grade Auditing. The R6 bank is composed of what he calls GPMs, or Goals-Problems-Masses.

GPMs are electronic entities the person has acquired through centuries of implanting. Each implant consists of an electronic "charge" paired with verbal phrases that must be listed and audited in order to erase that part of the mind.

The R6 bank *has mass and weight and occupies a space roughly fifteen feet in front of the preclear,* Hubbard reveals. *When one stops to consider that none of this ever occurs to psychiatrists, one wonders...one wonders....*[104]

In order to audit on that grade, called Grade Six in Scientology, one asks oneself the following question while connected to the E-meter—"What am I dramatizing?"

The person writes down the answer, as well as its opposite, on a list and continues asking the question until he can't think of any more items. All must be in the form of nouns.

For example, a Grade Six list might look like the following:

Girlness	Ungirlness
Smartness	Stupidness
Fatness	Thinness
Lateness	Earliness
Kindness	Meanness, etc.

It's widely believed that this level is dangerous, as the person is dealing with the core of his mind. It is, like the core of a nuclear reactor, *hot stuff.* Hubbard stresses the danger of that auditing level when he states in a bulletin, *Running a GPM badly can be quite deadly.*[105]

---

[104] Hubbard bulletin *From the Inner Structure of the Mind,* p. 2

[105] Hubbard bulletin *Solo Auditing and R6 EW,* p. 5

The preclear is finished with this level *when he knows he is no longer dramatizing.* The cost of this and the next level will be several thousand dollars.

The listing process on the Solo Course may continue for hundreds of hours, as the person maps out phrases that he believes are contained in his reactive mind. By this point, a Scientologist has a seriously endangered sense of reality.

An example of that is a drill performed on this level called TR 8-Q, a drill for Solo Auditor training.

In the drill, the person sits on a chair facing another chair on which an ashtray is placed. The drill is to train him to deliver thought into an object. He asks several questions of the ashtray, first verbally, then nonverbally, then verbally but with nonverbal intention. The questions asked of the ashtray are:

"Are you an ashtray?"
"Are you made of glass?"
"Are you sitting there?"
"Are you a corner?" (asked of every corner of the ashtray)[106]

The voyage into unreality continues on the final course of the lower levels of Scientology, the Clearing Course. Attaining the level of Clear is the goal of every Scientologist, because, once Clear, he will be ready for the mysterious, exciting, advanced levels of Scientology, called the OT levels, for Operating Thetan. On those levels, the person supposedly regains his long-lost powers of telepathy, telekinesis, etc., as well as the ability to travel at will outside his body, known in Scientology as *exteriorization.*

On the Clearing Course, Hubbard gives the exact pattern of the core of the reactive mind:

Part A—The 7s

---

[106] Hubbard bulletin *TR 8-Q Drill for Solo Auditor Training*

Part B—The Basic End Words
Part C—The Confusion GPM
Part D—The Objects—hollow
Part E—The Objects—solid

Each set of those parts A through E is called a "run," and there are ten runs to be completed to fully erase the reactive mind.

The preclear, seated at a table and connected to the E-meter, takes a series of prewritten lists by Hubbard and reads each item on the list to himself, watching the E-meter for *reads,* a movement of the needle on the E-meter's dial, as each item is read. He continues until there are no more reactions on the E-meter.

Occasionally, he's given the instruction to, "Spot the thetan," or "Spot the light," at which time he must look out in front of himself and "spot" a light in his "space."

Examples of the lists given in the 7s are:

To be nobody—to be everybody
To be me—to be you
To be myself—to be others
To be an animal—to be animals
To be a body—to be bodies
To be matter—to be space
To be a spirit—to be spirits
To be a god—to be gods
To do nothing—to do everything
To do much—to do little
To do it all—to do not any
To do ambitiously—to do slightingly
To have nothing—to have everything
To have much—to have little
To have all—to have none
To have hugely—to have poorly
To stay everywhere—to stay nowhere
To stay here—to stay there
To stay near—to stay far
To stay up—to stay down

Why his particular process is called the 7s is not known. In the next part of the Clearing process, the person is given another list of words by Hubbard that he must read to himself while watching the E-meter for reads. There are twenty-one items on the list:

The Now
The Past
The Future
The Time
The Space
The Motion
The Energy
The Masses
The Self
The Others
Life
Existence
Conditions
Effects
Pictures
Mind
Histories
Reaction
The Goal
Chaos
Universe

To do Part C of the Clearing process, the person adds the prefaces, "Creating to destroy...." And "Destroying to create...." To each of the twenty-one items in Part B. Again, the person audits himself on these new items using the E-meter.

In the fourth and fifth parts of the Clearing process, a person is given pictures of a series of objects, including triangles, circles, squares, ellipses, tetrahedrons, boxes, cubes, eggs, prisms, etc. The person must visualize those objects either coming at him or moving away from him in space while he marks down the reactions on the E-meter.

The person first visualizes one of each of the given objects in front of him, then two to either side of his face, then three to his front and sides, then four on either side and at front and back.

It's a testament to the efficacy of the hypnotic conditioning and mind control in Scientology that thousands of Scientologists have spent hundreds of hours on those drills, blindly obeying Hubbard and disregarding any inner instincts warning them they are engaged in the pursuit of folly.

The Scientologist will spend hundreds of hours and thousands of dollars in such auditing, until the time when he completes the "ten runs" necessary to "clear" him, or until he feels that his bank, or reactive mind, has "blown."

At that point, he is checked on the E-meter by an Examiner to verify that he has, indeed, "gone Clear."

Hubbard once wrote a sample advertisement for the state of Clear:

Do You Want More Out of Life?
Become a Scientology "Clear"
A Scientology "Clear" has:
Over 135 IQ
Creative imagination
Amazing vitality
Deep relaxation
Good memory
Strong willpower
Radiant health
Magnetic personality
Good self-control
If you would like to have all these qualities,
then look into Scientology.
Enquire today.

Today in Scientology organizations around the world, Scientologists are sitting in small rooms, holding two soup cans attached to their E-meters, staring into space, looking for the invisible objects Hubbard said are there. Soon, they will be "Clear."

And, if they have their way, so, one day, will you.

CHAPTER SEVEN

OT—Through the Wall of Fire and Beyond

Take our own bodies. I believe they are composed of myriads and myriads of infinitesimally small individuals, each in itself a unit of life, and that these units work in squads—or swarms, as I prefer to call them—and these infinitesimally small units live forever. When we die these swarms of units, like a swarm of bees, so to speak, betake themselves elsewhere, and go on functioning in some other form or environment.

Thomas Edison[107]

Hitler was involved in the same black magic and the same occult practices that my father was. The identical ones. Brainwashing is nothing compared to it. The proper term would be "soul cracking." It's like cracking open the soul, which then opens various doors to the

---

[107] Corydon, p. 356

power that exists, the satanic
and demonic powers.

(You take drugs) in order to
reach that state where you can,
quite literally, like a psychic
hammer, break their soul, and
pull the power through. He
(Hubbard) designed his
Scientology Operating Thetan
techniques to do the same thing.

It takes a couple of
hundred hours of auditing and
megathousands of dollars for the
privilege of having your head
turned into a glass Humpty
Dumpty—shattered into a million
pieces. It may sound like
incredible gibberish, but it made
my father a fortune.

L. Ron Hubbard, Jr., in
Penthouse magazine

An advertisement for the OT levels in a Scientology
magazine shows a dove flying high above a NASA-like
view of the earth. The ad reads:

As you progress in
Scientology, you start moving up
and out of the traps of this planet
and this universe.

For the first time in man's
long and black history, a being
can find freedom and knowledge
within one lifetime.

The key is to keep moving
on The Bridge.

At the upper levels of
Scientology, you'll learn the
secrets of this sector of the

universe, and the factors that
have trapped beings for countless
eons. Learn the technology that
will make it impossible for you
ever to be trapped again.[108]

The concept of OT is an important part of the cosmology of Scientology, as it is the promises made for the OT levels that motivate many members of Scientology to remain in the organization and work their way up The Bridge.

The concept of OT is similar in many ways to that of the *Ubermensch,* a term used by Hitler to signify the superior Aryan man, the superman. In Scientology cosmology, eons ago, at the beginning of this universe, we existed as thetans but possessed superior psychic powers that were native to us in that state. Over the centuries, as we became involved in the physical universe (called the MEST universe by Scientologists, after the acronym for Matter, Energy, Space, and Time—the elements, according to Hubbard, of the physical universe), we gradually lost our superhuman abilities, as we became involved with physical bodies and were subjected to the crippling electronic incidents known in Scientology as *implants.*

According to Scientology, in the beginning thetans together created the physical universe, but, as time passed, they became trapped within their own creation. Over the ages, as they took on various physical forms, they gradually lost awareness of their identity as thetans. The superhuman gods of ages past deteriorated into the degraded mortals of the present.

Enter Scientology. For the first time in recorded history, Hubbard promised his followers that a way had

---

[108] Scientology magazine, *It's Time to Improve Your Life: Your Guide to Scientology Services*

been found to restore to human beings both the awareness of their true identity as thetans and the once-possessed superhuman abilities, known in Scientology as OT abilities, an acronym for Operating Thetan.

However, only after the reactive mind has been erased in the Clear is it possible to rehabilitate the thetan and to restore those ancient powers. That auditing takes place on the OT levels, the mysterious and secret upper levels of Scientology.

The OT levels, and the OTs who are on them, are highly regarded by Scientologists still on the lower grades. The awe inspired by OTs in Scientology is somewhat like the respect given to PhDs in a university setting, but with an added aura of religious reverence.

On the OT levels, Hubbard promised, one learns the long-lost secrets *of this sector of the universe,* secrets of our past available for the first time in millions of years. By understanding those secrets and by doing the auditing on the upper levels, one can at last achieve freedom from the physical universe in which we have been trapped for so long.

The materials on those levels are a matter of extreme secrecy within Scientology. Over the years, the material from most of these levels has been made public, with the exception of the highest level to be released so far—OT VIII. At present, that level is administered in a floating classroom aboard a Scientology ship sailing the Caribbean. Because of elaborate security measures taken aboard the ship, the contents of that level remain a secret to those outside Scientology.

The following is a chart of the OT levels, the promises made for each, and the price of each, quoted from a recent Scientology magazine.

The OT Levels

OT VIII	Ability to be at cause knowingly and at will over thought, life, form, matter,	$8,000

	energy, space and time, subjective and objective	
OT VII	Rehabilitation of intention; ability to project intention	$5,100
OT VI	Ability to operate freely as a thetan exterior and to act pan-determinedly; extends the influence of the thetan to the universe of others	$9,600
OT V	Refamiliarizes a thetan exterior with the physical universe; freedom from fixed introversion into matter, energy space, time	$9,300 per 12.5 hrs
OT IV	Certainty of self as a being	$8,100 per 12.5 hrs
OT III	Return of full self-determinism; Freedom from overwhelm	$8,910
OT II	Ability to confront Whole Track	$5,225
OT I	Extroverts a being and brings about an awareness of himself as a thetan in relation to others and the physical universe	$2,750

Prices taken from *Source Magazine* (a Scientology magazine), issue 77, November 1991.

The cost of enlightenment isn't cheap in Scientology. The constant need for large sums of money in Scientology motivates many members to start their own businesses in an attempt to raise the funds needed to "go OT." Others may join the organization, committing themselves for the next billion years to the service of Scientology, in order to receive the free auditing given to staff members.

The route to immortality begins with OT I, a short level done soon after the person is Clear. That level consists of just one command. The Scientologist is instructed to go to a place where there are a lot of people, such as a park or mall, and to "Spot a person" repeatedly until a "cognition" occurs. At one time, that level was offered for $300 dollars. Currently, the price has jumped by a factor of nine.

Once the person has the requisite cognition, which is usually some kind of awareness of himself "as a thetan," as separate from all other thetans, he's ready to progress to OT Level II.

On Level II, an idea is introduced that existed as early as the Dianetics book in 1950, but it now becomes central—the idea of "entities." In Dianetics, Hubbard referred to the idea of *circuits* or *demon circuits,* the existence of disparate entities attached to a person. That belief comes into its own on the OT levels.

Although on the Clearing Course, the person has theoretically audited out his own reactive mind, on OT II he now has to deal with the reactive minds of those beings, or demons, attached to him. It's done in much the same way as on the Solo and Clearing courses.

On OT II, Hubbard gives a series of tables of GPMs, or implants, which must now be audited. The first list is:

Electrical GPM
Tocky GPM
Big Being GPM
House GPM
Psycho GPM
Banky GPM
Forerunner GPM
The Arrow
Double Rod
Woman
White Black Sphere
Hot Cold
Laughter-Calm
Dance Mob
Basic-Basic GPM

Basic GPM
The Command GPM
Lower LP GPM
LP GPM
Body GPM
Lower Bank, etc. [109]

The student is given an explanation for each of these "incidents." The instructions for auditing them are the same as on the Clearing Course. Each of the items is read aloud to oneself, and the E-meter reads marked down until the item no longer reads.

The explanation for the *Electrical GPM* states that *it has an electrical shock...to convince a thetan he should think of himself as an electrical being.* The date of this implant is given by Hubbard as *210,000,866[th].* Various commands are given to audit, including:

Create (shock)
Create no (shock)
Destroy (shock)
Destroy no (shock)
Love (shock)
Love no (shock)[110]

The Laughter-Calm GPM, or implant, is described as having taken place 19,760 trillion years ago.

> This takes place in a cave.
> It is 7-1/8ths of a second in
> duration. It has screams of
> laughter, very wild, and calm....
>
> It is a pole with a split in it.
> Laughter comes from the rear
> half and calm from the front half
> simultaneously. Then they

---

[109] Hubbard, *OT Course—Section Two,* p. 2

[110] Ibid, p. 3

> reverse. It gives one a sensation
> of total disagreement. The trick is
> to conceive of both at the same
> time. This tends to knock one
> out....[111]

The Dance Mob GPM is given as occurring 18,992 trillion years ago.

> The duration is 7/8ths of a
> second. There is a pole that pulls
> one in. One is caught on the
> pole. The actual incident is in
> connecting with this thing and
> trying to get off it.
>
> The dancing comes after
> the actual incident, and consists
> of a mob dancing around one,
> chanting various things. In
> running this, get the phrases
> that are chanted....[112]

The third OT level, OT III, known in Scientology as the Wall of Fire, is the level to which Scientologists look forward most eagerly, for it is on this level that Hubbard promises they will at last learn the great secret of this sector of the universe. A great deal of mythology surrounds this level. According to Hubbard, it is this long-lost secret that accounts for the current degraded condition of man. Once you know, "The secret of OT III," Hubbard promises, you'll then understand the world today and why it is the way it is.

Security is strictly enforced on this level. The OT III materials are kept in a locked room in the Advanced Organizations. When carried outside the organization, they must always be kept in a locked briefcase, and the

---

[111] Hubbard, *OT Course—Part One*, p. 23

[112] Ibid, p. 23

contents never revealed to anyone outside the organization or even to anyone inside it but not yet on that level.

However, the highly guarded secret materials on this level have been made public by several sources. We now know that "the great secret of this sector of the universe," as revealed to Scientology students, is as follows:

The head of the Galactic Confederation (76 planets around larger stars visible from here) (founded 95,000,000 years ago, very space opera) solved overpopulation (250 billion or so per planet—178 billion on average) by mass implanting.

He caused people to be brought to Teegeeack (Earth) and put an H Bomb on the principal volcanoes (incident 2) and then the Pacific ones were taken in boxes to Hawaii, and the Atlantic ones to Las Palmas and there "packaged."

His name was Xenu. He used renegades. Various misleading data by means of circuits, etc., was placed in the implants.

When through with his crime, Loyal Officers (to the people) captured him after six years of battle and put him in an electronic mountain trap where he still is. "They" are gone. The place (Confed.) has since been a desert.

The length and brutality of

it all was such that this
Confederation never recovered.
The implant is calculated to kill
(by pneumonia, etc.) anyone who
attempts to solve it. This liability
has been dispensed with by my
tech development.

One can free wheel
through the implant and die
unless it is approached as
precisely outlined. The "free
wheel" (auto running on and on)
lasts too long, denies sleep, etc.,
and one dies.

In December, '67, I knew
somebody had to take the
plunge. I did and emerged very
knocked out but alive. Probably
the only one ever to do so in
75,000,000 years. I have all the
data now but only that given here
is needful.

Good luck.[113]

In subsequent OT III bulletins, Hubbard explains
further. Millions of years ago, an evil dictator of the
Galactic Federation decided to solve the overpopulation
problem in this galaxy by rounding up people, freezing
them, and shipping them to earth on spaceships. They
were deposited on two volcanoes, one at Las Palmas, one
in Hawaii. Then nuclear explosions were set off, blowing
the frozen souls into the stratosphere, where they were
collected by "electronic ribbons," or force fields, and
brought back to earth, where they were packaged into
"clusters."

---

[113] Hubbard, *Operating Thetan Section Three*, p. 1

After packaging, they were subjected to implants, in which they were shown many different scenes on huge screens. Then they were released.

And so, according to Hubbard, the great secret of this sector of the universe is that each person on earth isn't just a single person but a collection, or cluster, of hundreds of different entities.

That places all earlier auditing in Scientology in a different perspective. The real goal of auditing up to Clear has been to isolate the dominant entity (the "I") from the pack and clear him first.

The entities attached to the person are called body thetans in Scientology. On OT III, the Scientologist learns how to—while connected to the E-meter—locate and contact these invisible entities and to audit them through the nuclear explosion and implant that occurred 75,000,000 years ago. As a result, according to Hubbard, the entity becomes free to fly off and live a life of its own.

To do this, the Scientologist, alone in a locked room, hooked up to an E-meter, telepathically locates an "entity" attached to some part of his body. He asks the entity telepathically which volcano he was taken to, Las Palmas or Hawaii, while watching for reads on the E-meter.

He must telephathically audit the entity through "Incident Two," which includes the following sequence:

H-bomb dropped on volcano
Explosion
Terrific winds
Thetan carried over peak
Electronic ribbon came up
He stuck to it
It was then pulled down, and he was implanted with R6[114]

---

[114] Ibid, p. 24

If the entity does not "leave" after auditing him on Incident Two, then it is necessary to audit this entity on an earlier implant that occurred 4 quadrillion years ago, called "Incident One," and which consists of:

Loud snap
Waves of light
Chariot comes out, turns right and left
Cherub comes out
Blows horn, comes close
Shattering series of snaps
Cherub fades back (retreats)
Blackness dumped on thetan[115]

Because Hubbard says that each person on earth has hundreds of body thetans, Scientologists can spend a hundred hours or more auditing on OT III. The result, in theory, of being freed from all one's body thetans is that one should be able to "exteriorize," or go out of one's body at will. Although many Scientologists claim that ability, there is in Scientology no objective test to determine if the ability has ever been achieved.

The purpose of the remaining OT levels is to reorient the "newly exteriorized thetan" with the physical universe, and, through a series of drills, help him regain his long-lost powers.

On OT IV, the Scientologist practices "mocking up" (mentally recreating) implants and GPMs until he is "proofed against any possibility of being reimplanted" now that he has finished running implants on OT III.[116]

On OT V, the "thetan exterior" is "refamiliarized with the physical universe in order to increase his ability to communicate with the environment.... He learns to use his new abilities as a thetan with wisdom and judgment."

---

[115] Ibid, p. 24

[116] Hubbard, *OT IV Solo*

OT V, subtitled *Cause Over MEST,* contains a series of drills, done while the person is lying down with eyes closed:

> Spot a spot in the room.
> Spot a spot in your body. (These are done alternately until a "cognition" is reached.)
>
> Spot a spot outside. Spot a spot on the sun.

In other drills on this level:

> The pre-OT is to pick out an object ahead of him and wrap an energy beam around it and himself and pull himself toward the object with shortening of the beam.
>
> Notice what happens.
>
> Locate an object, draw energy from it into you. Repeat at least ten times.
>
> Notice a cloud and notice the space between you and it.
>
> Notice the motion of the earth and your relationship to it.
>
> Notice something about ten people.[117]

OT VI consists of more drills to "rehabilitate the thetan," including:

> Be three feet in back of your head. Whatever you are looking at, copy it a dozen times, put it into you. Find the two back corners of the room and hold

---

[117] Hubbard, *OT V—Cause Over MEST*

onto them without thinking for two minutes.

Find two corners of the planet Earth, hold onto them for two minutes.

Find a place where you are not.

Spot three spots on your body.

Spot three spots in the room.

Be in the following places: The room, the sky, the moon, the sun.

Locate an animal. Postulate him moving from one spot to another. Observe him doing this.

Find a man walking. Postulate his walking faster. Do this with 20 people.

Find a person in a distant land. Notice the time of day. Notice the terrain. Notice the general environment. Smell the air. Locate a thought that is his. Locate a thought that is yours.

Postulate anger, boredom, grief, cheerfulness, and serenity in that order. This is continued until you are sure that you can create any emotion.

Exteriorized, visit a friend who lives in another state. Greet him and flow affinity to him. Ask him to communicate to you by letter.[118]

OT VII has to do with "rehabilitating the intention of the thetan." On this level, the person practices psychically placing his "intention" into another person or object:

> Find some plants, trees, etc., and communicate to them individually until you know they received your communication.
>
> Go to a zoo or a place with many types of life and communicate with each of them until you know the communication is received, and, if possible, returned.
>
> Go out to a park, train station, or other busy area. Practice placing an intention into individuals until you can successfully and easily place an intention into or on a being and/or a body.[119]

Since no one outside of Scientology has seen the contents of OT VIII, one can only wonder what might be in this secret level, the end result of which is to become completely "at cause" over the physical universe.

The OT levels have changed somewhat over time. However, there is more that is unchanged than changed.

Other than the time and money expended in pursuit of the ambiguous goals promised for each of these levels, is there any danger in these drills?

Yes, say researchers.

---

[118] Hubbard, *OT VI*

[119] Hubbard, *OT VII Rundown*

In a study of the psychological effects of several different cults, psychologists Conway and Siegelman found that:

> hour for hour,
> Scientology's techniques may be
> more than twice as dangerous as
> those of any other major cult....
> On the average, former
> Scientologists surveyed reported
> more than twice the combined
> negative effects of all other cult
> groups. Some of the negative
> effects observed among former
> Scientologists were: sexual
> dysfunction, violent outbursts,
> hallucinations and delusions,
> and suicidal or self-destructive
> tendencies.[120]

Dr. John Clark of Harvard University agrees, stating that, as with all cults, many former Scientologists have experienced severe mental breakdowns:

> Even if members do leave
> the group, it may take months or
> even years for them to regain lost
> intellectual powers and their
> sense of well-being.... To me, the
> latest casualties of these
> extended manipulations are
> nearly unbearable to
> contemplate. More tortured
> rejects are beginning to straggle
> home because they are useless to
> (Scientology) now. Some are

---

[120] Conway, Flo and Siegelman, Jim, *Information Disease: Have Cults Created a New Mental Illness?*

> simply chronically psychotic,
> while others...cannot control the
> content of their minds enough to
> work out their life problems....[121]

In the Lewis Carroll-like world of Scientology, and especially on the OT levels, a person might well wonder if he has gone "through the looking glass," so bizarre are those levels.

Why do people in Scientology go along with those levels?

"It's kind of like *The Emperor's New Clothes*," one former Scientologist explains.

> Nobody wants to be the
> one who says the emperor has no
> clothes on.

> But it's other things, too.
> You believe that Hubbard is
> right, that he is like God. You
> believe that if he says it's true,
> then it's true. And, too, because
> everything is so expensive, you
> just assume that it has value.
> After spending a few thousand
> dollars on Scientology, no one
> wants to admit that he's been
> had....[122]

It is interesting that the goals of both Hitler and Hubbard were the same: to create a new race of supermen (and women)—Hitler through genetic breeding, and Hubbard through auditing.

---

[121] Rudin, Marcia, *The Cult Phenomenon: Fad or Fact?*

[122] Affidavit of an unnamed (by choice) ex-member of Scientology

Two men, born of the same occult crucible, who have wrought untold destruction in the lives of those whose paths they happened to cross.

It is reported that Scientology has allocated half a million dollars in a special trust to ensure that the name of L. Ron Hubbard will live on forever.

Whether he will live on in fame or in infamy remains to be seen.

CHAPTER EIGHT

The Language of Scientology—ARC, SPs, PTPs, and BTs

> The language of the totalist environment is characterized by the thought-terminating cliché. The most far-reaching and complex of human problems are compressed into brief, highly reductive, definitive-sounding phrases, easily memorized and easily expressed. These become the start and finish of any ideological analysis. In thought reform, for instance, the phrase "bourgeois mentality" is used to encompass and critically dismiss ordinarily troublesome concerns like the quest for individual expression, the exploration of alternative ideas, and the search for perspective and balance.... (loaded language is) the "language of non-thought."
>
> *Thought Reform and the Psychology of Totalism,* by Robert Jay Lifton

Two Scientologists meet on the street.

"How're you doing?" one asks the other.

"Well, to tell the truth, I've been a bit out ruds because of a PTP with my second dynamic because of some bypassed charge having to do with my MEST at her apartment. When I moved in, I gave her an R-factor, and I thought we were in ARC about it, but lately, she seems to have gone a bit PTS, so I recommended she see the MAA at the AO to blow some charge and get her ethics in.

"He gave her a review to F/N and VGIs, but she did a roller coaster, so I think there's an SP somewhere on her lines. I tried to audit her myself, but she had a dirty needle and BIs and was acting really 1.1, so I finally sent her to Qual to spot the entheta on her lines. Other than that, everything's fine."

There is no Scientologist anywhere to whom that explanation wouldn't make perfect sense. Like a secret code, the language of Scientology helps members identify and bond with each other and creates an invisible but effective boundary between the cult and the world "outside."

There are many cults that use the loaded language described by Lifton—the language of nonthought—but there is probably no other cult in which the manipulation of the cult member through language is achieved as completely or with as much sophistication as in Scientology.

As anyone in the advertising world knows, if you want to control a person's behavior, you must first control his thought. Hubbard did that in Scientology through the prolific propaganda in written bulletins, tapes, and films to which members are constantly exposed.

A more subtle form of thought control was achieved by Hubbard through the creation of a new language— Scientologese—used and understood only within the cult.

How is thought restricted by the language in Scientology? In several ways. Many of the new words are formed by changing the part of speech of an existing noun, usually from a verb or adjective into a noun. The nouns used in Scientology have black-and-white, concrete meanings. There are no shades of gray in the Scientology vocabulary.

Scientology makes extensive use of acronyms and abbreviations, but modifiers are almost nonexistent. One could probably exist for ten years in Scientology without ever using an adverb or adjective.

Most nouns in Scientology have only one meaning. Gone are the variegated definitions and idiomatic uses of regular English nouns. Many of the terms in Scientology have come from the computer and engineering fields and have precise definitions that leave little to the imagination. When common English words are given a new meaning in Scientology, the older, multiple meanings have been dropped in favor of a single, concrete, Scientology meaning.

Hubbard was fond of transforming verbs—words of action—into more static nouns. Examples include:

"Assist," which means to help, becomes "an assist," one of the auditing processes of Scientology, e.g., "Would you like me to give you an assist?"

The verb "to be" is turned into a noun in the Scientology word "beingness." Similarly transformed are "doingness," "havingness," knowingness," "rightness," "wrongness," "livingness," and "isness."

The noun, "between lives implant" comes from the English verb "to implant."

The verb "to confront" becomes a noun, "confront," e.g., "Doing training routines will increase a person's confront."

The verb "to motivate" becomes a noun in "motivator," e.g., "Bill pulled in a motivator when he had his accident."

"To postulate" becomes a noun in the Scientology word "postulate," e.g., "I have a postulate that I will win the lottery."

Even the word "clear" in Scientology has been transformed into a noun from the adjective of the same name.

Other Scientology nouns deriving from English verbs and adjectives are: "basic," "fall," "rise," "secondary," "overt," "overrun," "randomity," "processing," "read," "release," "review," and "static."

As an example of how thought is restricted in these English-to-Scientology transformations, the word "clear" in English had at least thirty different definitions—free of clouds, having no blemishes, free from guilt, passing without contact, making a profit, etc. In Scientology, the word "clear" has one very concrete meaning—a person who has completed the Clearing Course in Scientology.

Another example is the word "release," which in English has nine different definitions, including to set free, to let loose, to release from an obligation, to be set free from pain, to permit to be issued, etc. In Scientology, a "release" refers to one thing—someone who has completed one of the lower levels of Scientology auditing.

Acronyms and abbreviations are common in Scientology, again a way of abbreviating thought. Acronyms can be parts of the organization, as in the SO (Sea Organization), GO (Guardian's Office), AO (Advanced Organization), ASHO (American Saint Hill Organization), and CMO (Commodore's Messenger Organization).

Or they can have to do with time, e.g., AD (After Dianetics) and BD (Before Dianetics). Years in Scientology are numbered in relation to the year 1950, the year the Dianetics book was published. Therefore, 1992, becomes AD 42 in Scientology. The year 1940 becomes BD 10.

There are many acronyms that have to do with the "technical" processes of auditing, such as BIs (bad indicators), VGIs (very good indicators), C/S (case supervisor), F/N (floating needle), BPC (bypassed charge), TA (tone arm action), EP (end phenomena), TR (training routine), and S&D (search and discovery), to name a few.

Acronyms can refer to things you can be—SP (suppressive person), PTS (potential trouble source), OT (operating thetan), PC (preclear), and HAS (Hubbard Apprentice Scientologist). They can also refer to things you can have—PTP (present-time problem), OW (Overt and withhold), 2D (second dynamic), ARC (affinity, reality, and communication), MEST (material things, from matter, energy, space, and time).

An acronym can be something to read, such as an HCOB (Hubbard Communication Office Bulletin) or HCOPL (Hubbard Communication Office Policy Letter). It can be something you can do, as in Q&A (question and answer, or to question a command). It can also be a person: CO (Commanding Officer), MAA (Master at Arms or Ethics Officer), D of T (Director of Training), D of P (Director of Processing), or "wog," (worthy Oriental gentleman, meaning anyone not a Scientologist).

Many of the words in Scientology are simply shortened, rendering thought even less necessary than it already was: "ack" (acknowledgement), "admin" (administration), "tech" (technical), "qual" (qualifications), "inval" (invalidation), "eval" (evaluation), "org" (organization), "ruds" (rudiments), "R-factor" (reality factor), "sec" (security), "demo" (demonstration), and "E-meter" (electropsychometer).

Of the many new words created by Hubbard in Scientology, the majority are composed of two words taken from regular English and combined to create a new word in Scientology. Some of the completely new words can be traced to their English origins.

Examples of these new words, and their meanings, are:

Aberee—one who is aberrated

Anaten—a state of being unconscious to some degree

Anchor points—a person's boundaries in space

Alter-is—to consciously change something

Analytical mind—the conscious mind, which, without the influence of the reactive mind, operates logically

As-is—to make something disappear by staring at it for a long time

Awareness of the awareness unit—another word for the person

Bad indicators—a person not smiling and not having a "floating needle" after a session

Between lives area—a word to describe the events that happen between the time a person dies and when he gets his next body

Bypassed charge—emotions restimulated during auditing but not discharged

Case gain—progress made by an individual because of auditing

Case supervisor—the person who examines each session done by the auditor and programs the next session

Clay demo—a picture made in clay to demonstrate the learning of a theory

Comm Course—the Communications Course in Scientology

Comm lag—a long hesitation in conversation

Comm line—the imaginary line between two people who are talking together

Covert hostility—a condition of masked anger

Cycle of action—defined by Hubbard as start, change, stop

Degraded being—a person in really bad shape

Destimulate—to calm down the reactive mind

Dirty needle—a certain motion of the needle on an E-meter that is ragged and erratic

Eighth dynamic—the Scientology term for God

Enmest—short for "enturbulated MEST," which means anything material that is in a disorganized state

Entheta—short for "enturbulated theta," a person or thing that is destructive and upset, usually referring to someone or something against Scientology

Enturbulate—to upset

First dynamic—things having to do with the person himself

Floating needle—a needle on the E-meter that is lazily floating back and forth across the dial, indicating that nothing in the reactive mind is activated at that moment

Genetic entity—the identity of the body containing a consciousness of evolution

Itsa—a person who, in auditing, is identifying something

Line charge—a prolonged spell of uncontrolled laughter.

Mental image pictures—pictures in the mind; memories

Misemotion—any painful or unpleasant emotion

Missed withhold—something bad a person did that someone else found out about

Not is—to make something that exists into nothing

Obnosis—observation of the obvious

Operating thetan—a person minus the reactive mind who has the ability to control the physical universe

Overt motivator sequence—what happens when someone does something bad, then subconsciously causes something bad to happen to himself

Reach and withdraw—a principle in Scientology that something reached for tends to withdraw, and vice versa

Reactive mind—the subconscious mind, which, according to Dianetic theory, accounts for illogical behavior in humans

Restimulate—to stir up the contents of the reactive mind

Second dynamic—having to do with love relationships, sex, and marriage

Stable datum—something known to be true upon which other facts can be based

Terminal of comparable magnitude—something or someone equal in some quality with another

Theta—the life force, spirit, or soul

Thetan—the person as a spiritual being or soul

Theta trap—any place that attracts people

Third dynamic—having to do with the group

Third party—the Scientology principle that in any conflict between two people, there's a third person who is the real cause of the problem

Time track—the recorded history of a person's lives back to the beginning of time

Tone arm—one of the dials on the E-meter that shows how much "charge" has been erased in the session

Tone scale—a scale of emotions in Scientology

Two-way comm—conversation between two people

Unmock—to destroy or make nothing of something

Upstat—someone who has high statistics; the opposite of "downstat"

Uptone—someone who is at a high emotional tone level; the opposite of "downtone"

Very good indicators—what happens after an auditing session, when the preclear is smiling and has a floating needle

Those are just a few of the new words in Scientology.

The final category of language in Scientology has to do with words that are appropriated directly from English and are given new meanings within the framework of Scientology. Although the original word in English may have had a variety and shades of meaning, the new Scientology meaning will be unique and concrete.

The word "affinity" in English can refer to either a physical or emotional closeness. In Scientology, "affinity" is used to replace the word "love" and its many connotations. "Love" isn't used in Scientology. "Affinity" means a willingness to be close to and share the same space with, or a liking for someone.

"Affinity" is also one of the components of the "ARC triangle," together with "reality" and "communication." The theory in Scientology is that if any one of the three corners of the triangle is increased, the result will be greater ARC or understanding.

In English, the word "agreement" can have many meanings, such as the act of agreeing, an understanding, or a contract. In Scientology, the word means the agreement of two or more people about reality, which is said to exist only when there is agreement that it exists.

In English, an auditor is one who checks the bookkeeping and finances of an organization. In Scientology, it means one who delivers the processes of auditing to a preclear, the Scientology version of a counselor.

To a person outside Scientology, the bank is the place one goes for money. In Scientology, the word "bank" is a slang term for the reactive mind and is commonly used as an adjective meaning irrational or unpleasant, as in, "The children are acting really banky today."

There was once a sport in England called "bullbaiting," in which several dogs would tease or attack a bull. Hubbard appropriated that term for a different purpose. In Scientology, "bullbaiting" refers to the Training Routine, or drill, in which one person tries to provoke another to react, while the person being provoked attempts to maintain a perfect, unblinking stare.

Before Scientology, a "button" was something that held a shirt together. In Scientology, it refers to any words or ideas that cause someone to react or that make him uncomfortable. For example, a short person might have a button about being short, or a fat person about being fat. The purpose of the drill TR-0 Bullbaited is to locate and "flatten" a person's buttons.

A "case" may have meant many things before Scientology—a legal argument, a person being treated by a social worker, a container in which to carry something, or a full box of beer. In Scientology, a "case" refers to one thing—a person's reactive mind being restimulated. A person undergoing Scientology auditing is frequently told, "Don't discuss your case with anyone."

A "chain" in English can be either a series of connected links, or a more symbolic series of connected circumstances or events. In Scientology, a "chain" has to do with a group of pictures in the reactive mind that have a physical characteristic in common, e.g., "Today we'll audit your stomach-pains chain."

"Charge" in English has a variety of meanings—what one does with a credit card, to add an electrical current to, to attack or move forward, to entrust with the care of someone, to make an accusation, or the instruction or verdict by a jury. In Scientology, however, "charge" refers to the harmful energy or force stored in the reactive mind.

Different people can have charge on different items or subjects, e.g., "He has a lot of charge on women."

"Ethics" is a complicated subject in the regular world. It's defined as *the study of standards of conduct and moral judgment.* In Scientology, "ethics" refers to the disciplinary branch of the organization and to Hubbard's policies that govern the activities of that branch. Most Scientologists have a certain amount of fear of "ethics." An example of its use would be, "If you don't get your stats (statistics) up, you'll be sent to ethics."

The word "dynamic" is an example of an adjective turned into a noun. In English, "dynamic" means the opposite of "static," but in Scientology, it refers to the eight arbitrary divisions of life Hubbard devised. For example, the first dynamic refers to the person himself; the second dynamic to the sexual relationships, marriage, and family; the third dynamic to the group, etc. Although that word can be used as a noun in English, the meaning is somewhat different.

The word "static" is also altered from adjective into noun in Scientology, where it refers to the thetan or soul. In Scientology, a "static" is defined as a being without mass, wavelength, time, or position.

"Indicators" in Scientology refer to specific characteristics of the preclear during auditing—whether he's smiling, the color of his skin, and whether he has good eye contact. In Scientology, there can be good indicators (GIs), very good indicators (VGIs), bad indicators (BIs), or very bad indicators (VBIs).

A "process" in Scientology refers to a specific auditing action done on a preclear.

"Raw meat" in Scientology isn't something one cooks for dinner. It refers to the person walking through the door who's never before had Scientology auditing and who is a prospect for Scientology services.

The word "reality" undergoes an interesting transformation in Scientology. It changes from a word that means "that which is" in English to "that which is agreed upon" in Scientology. In other words, in Scientology, unless there's agreement that something exists, it doesn't. All reality, according to Scientology, has been created by agreement. The physical universe exists only because at some point in the past, thetans agreed together that it did.

According to Scientology theory, as soon as thetans agree together that the universe no longer exists, it will cease to exist.

A "lock" in English can be something that keeps a door from being opened. In Scientology, the word refers to a somewhat-painful emotional experience, though it doesn't, however, contain actual physical pain or unconsciousness.

A "terminal" to most people might mean the display component of a computer or a Greyhound bus station. To a Scientologist, a "terminal" is a person at a particular spot or doing a particular job. The word can be loosely used to mean, simply, a person, e.g., "Go give this letter to the appropriate terminal."

Other words that have a specific Scientology meaning include:

Ally—someone who isn't really your friend in Scientology.

Circuit—something that is only in one's head.

Mass—mental entities having actual physical mass.

Roller coaster—someone whose emotional condition goes up and down.

Rudiments—asking a person at the beginning of auditing if they have any ARC breaks (upsets), present-time problems, or missed withholds. If so, the person has "out-ruds," which must be corrected before auditing can begin.

Session—the precise period of time during which auditing takes place.

Significance—the phrases embedded in the person's reactive mind as a result of implants; also the ideas learned in a course of study.

Source—refers to Hubbard, the name by which he is most commonly known in Scientology.

Sympathy—a negative trait in Scientology, where one is trained not to feel sympathy for anyone.

Understanding—in Scientology, this consists of three things: affinity, reality, and communication. Increasing any of those three results in increased understanding. Conversely, lowering any of the three results in decreased understanding.

Valence—any identity a person happens to be in at the time. One can have many valences, e.g., "Whenever she's around her mother, she goes into the valence of her father."

One of the most difficult things about leaving Scientology is the problem of what to do about the language. Many ex-members report problems of thinking and even dreaming in Scientologese for months, sometimes years, after leaving the cult.

That can also pose a problem for someone trying to counsel a recent defector from Scientology. Not knowing the language can put the counselor at a disadvantage and prevent the counselee from feeling understood. The same holds true for family members trying to communicate with someone newly out of Scientology. Because they don't speak or understand the language, they can't reach the person they're trying to help.

Manipulation of language is a very real, powerful tool in the hands of a cult leader. By controlling language, the cult leader can control the thoughts, and, therefore, the lives, of those who have strayed into his fold.

Legally, there's nothing wrong with a man like Hubbard manipulating the thoughts and minds of others for the express purpose of exploiting them for his own profit. Mental rape isn't a crime.

Scientology, Hubbard once claimed, is the only game in the universe where everybody wins.

The victims of Scientology know better.

CHAPTER NINE

The Sea Org—"For the Next Billion Years"

All mass movements generate in their adherents readiness to die and a proclivity for action; all of them, irrespective of the doctrine they preach and the program they project, breed fanaticism, enthusiasm, fervent hope, hatred, and intolerance; all of them are capable of releasing a powerful flow of activity in certain departments of life; all of them demand blind faith and singlehearted allegiance.

The True Believer by Eric Hoffer

I, _____ DO HEREBY AGREE to enter into employment with the SEA ORGANIZATION and, being of sound mind, do fully realize and agree to abide by its purpose, which is to get ETHICS In on this PLANET AND UNIVERSE, and, fully and without reservation, subscribe to the discipline, mores, and conditions of this group and pledge to abide by them.

> THEREFORE, I CONTRACT
> MYSELF TO THE SEA
> ORGANIZATION FOR THE NEXT
> BILLION YEARS.

> (Contract of employment
> for the Sea Organization)

On the Scientology "upper level" called OT III, the Scientologist learns the great secret of "this sector of the universe," which is that 75,000,000 years ago, an evil dictator named Xenu, in an effort to solve the galaxy's overpopulation problem, shot and froze thousands of thetans, shipped them to earth, and glued them together in massive nuclear explosions on volcanoes in Hawaii and Las Palmas.

Actually, there was more to that story. Xenu's brigade of soldiers was called the Loyal Officers. After he finished implanting all the frozen souls blown up in the two volcanoes:

> the Loyal Officers revolted
> and captured Xenu. He was
> imprisoned in a mountaintop on
> planet Earth (on the island of
> Madeira) and placed inside a wire
> cage with an eternal battery
> (where he remains today). In the
> battle between the Loyal Officers
> and Xenu's renegades, most of
> these planets were turned into
> billiard balls. Earth was a
> radioactive cinder and became
> known as "The Evil Place."

That's why nobody ever comes here except renegades and criminals who were dumped here.

> The entire concept of the
> Sea Org was said by Hubbard to

be, "a regathering of Loyal
Officers." This time, he and his
most trusted officers wouldn't
fail. They would "decontaminate"
Earth, and later, this entire
sector of the Galaxy, from the
devastation inflicted by Xenu and
his renegades.[123]

The motto of the Sea Org is, "We Come Back." Every Sea Org member believes in his heart that he or she is a member of an ancient organization that once before tried, and failed, to save the earth.

They believe, as Hubbard told them, that this is their last chance. If they fail this time to rescue the planet from certain, impending nuclear devastation, it'll be too late. The souls on the planet will be doomed for trillions of years into the future.

Sea Org members believe themselves to be "the cream of the cream of Scientology." In a bulletin entitled, *The Sea Organization,* Hubbard wrote:

If almost any person in the
Sea Organization were to appear
in a Scientology group or Org, he
would be lionized, red-carpeted,
and Very-Important-Personed
beyond belief.

For the Sea Organization is
composed of the "aristocracy" of
Scientology.

These people, alone and on
their own, are all stars in the sky
of their areas.

It is like one of the old
regiments of gentlemen, where

---

[123] Corydon, p. 365-67

> any private would be, in another
> but common regiment, a
> colonel....
>
> The Sea Organization is
> composed of people who alone
> would excite great admiration,
> but who together, well-organized,
> can actually get the job done.
>
> And although our lowest
> deckhand could be a "duke," only
> all of us together could get on
> with the job.
>
> And that's how and
> why...the Sea Organization came
> into being and why we are
> here....

Life in the Sea Org has never been easy. Members work hours that would seem impossible to an ordinary mortal. Pay is low, rewards are few, but there's the satisfaction of knowing that one is working for the salvation of souls and the rescue of the planet.

"Stiff ethics" has always been the norm in the Sea Org. The practices of overwhelming security checks, confinement in chain lockers or bilge tanks, served on the ships as ethics remedies to bring the recalcitrant or dissatisfied into line. There's no reason to believe things are much different now.

Overboarding was begun by Hubbard after one of the Sea Org members on the *Apollo* mistakenly untied the wrong hawser, setting the huge ship adrift in a foreign harbor. That unfortunate person was immediately tossed over the side on Hubbard's order. From then on, overboarding became a regular practice on the ship.

One witness describes the practice:

> Students and crew were
> lined up on deck in the early

hours every morning. They
waited to hear whether they were
on the day's list of miscreants.
Those who knew they were would
remove their shoes, jackets, and
wristwatches in anticipation. The
drop was between fifteen and
forty feet, depending upon which
deck was used.

Sometimes, people were
blindfolded first, and either their
feet or hands loosely tied.
Nonswimmers were tied to a
rope. Being hurled such a
distance, blindfolded and
restrained, into cold seawater,
must have been terrifying. Worst
of all was the fear that you would
hit the side of the ship as you
fell, your flesh ripped open by
barnacles. Overboarding was a
very traumatic experience.[124]

The chain locker was a small compartment in the
bow of the ship where excess chain attached to the
anchor was wound up and stored. It was a cold, dark, wet
area frequently inhabited by rats. It was into that
compartment that people would be lowered as a form of
"ethics," or punishment. It was a dangerous form of
punishment, since at any moment the chain could be
released, and the person in the chain locker, if not
careful, would be caught in the outgoing chain.

In several cases, children were put into the chain
locker as punishment for misdeeds. In one case, Hubbard
ordered a five-year-old deaf-mute girl into the chain
locker "to cure her illness." In another case, a four-year-

---

[124] Atack, p. 187

old boy was kept in the chain locker for two weeks, because he ate some Telex tape. His mother was told that he was actually a very old thetan in a young body and shouldn't be given sympathy because of his body.[125]

That is a common conception of children in Scientology.

Another form of "ethics" on the ship had the person:

> put into old, rusty tanks,
> way below the ship, with filthy
> bilge water, no air, and hardly
> sitting height, for anything from
> twenty-four hours to a week,
> getting their oxygen via tubes.
> They were kept awake, often for
> days on end. They ate from the
> communal food bucket with their
> blistered and filthy hands. They
> chipped away at rust
> unceasingly. The Ethics Officers
> were constantly checking outside
> to hear if the hammering
> continued. There were no
> bathroom facilities in the bilge
> tanks....[126]

One report of life in the Sea Org on the ship comes from a teenager who joined Scientology with her parents in the 1970s. Her name is Tonja Burden, and she was separated from her parents and placed in the Cadet Organization in Los Angeles:

> the Cadet Organization
> consisted of two three-story
> buildings that housed

---

[125] Corydon, p. 25

[126] Atack, p. 180

approximately 400 children. The Cadet Organization was designed to teach children about Scientology. My duties were to care for, clean, and feed the children. Myself and another girl my age were the two oldest children at the Cadet Organization.

The living conditions were squalid. Glass from broken windows lay strewn over the floors. Live electrical wires were exposed in areas where young children played. We received little food. On several occasions, spoiled milk with maggots was served to the children. The maggots were removed by hand before the milk was served. In addition to caring for the children, I cleaned the toilets daily.

Children were not allowed to live with their parents. Scientology permitted one visit every other week, and only for forty-five minutes during mealtime....

I saw the *Apollo* for the first time and was greatly disappointed by its dilapidated condition. Once aboard, I was given a berth in the women's dorm and placed in the Estates Project Force (EPF).

In the EPF, my day began at 6:00 AM. I scrubbed clothes

from 6:00 AM until 12:00 noon without breakfast or any breaks. The clothes were scrubbed by hand in a bucket, and I was directed to rinse each article in thirteen separate buckets. Then I hung the clothes on the deck to dry.

After a one-half-hour lunch, I was assigned to clean six cabins. Cabins had to meet white-glove inspection. If the cabins weren't cleaned to white-glove perfection, I had to run a lap around the boat before recleaning the room. My day would end at about 12:00 midnight.

On rainy days, I ironed the clothes dry. This required ironing during the evening hours and into the morning hours. On many occasions, I ironed through the night, finishing at 6:00 AM. I then started washing the next morning's clothing.

On occasion, I worked three or four days without sleeping. I fell asleep at the ironing board with a hot iron in my hand. My senior caught me sleeping and yanked my head off the board. She ordered me to run laps and assigned me a condition of "Doubt." A condition of Doubt required fifteen hours of amends work. That additional work had to be performed during my sleep or mealtime.

While in the EPF, I never
heard from my parents, no phone
calls or letters. Aboard the ship, I
received a Telex informing me
that my father had been declared
an SP (Suppressive Person). They
said he was a spy within
Scientology. I began crying and
asked to leave, telling them I
could convince my father to
return to Scientology...but they
would not permit me to leave.

I was told to disconnect
from my parents, because they
were SPs. Disconnection meant
no more communication with my
parents. They told me my parents
would not make it in the world,
but that I would make it in the
world....[127]

Tonja finally escaped from Scientology by stealing
keys from a sleeping guard and crawling through an air
duct to freedom.

One of the most infamous aspects of the Sea Org is
the dreaded RPF, or "Rehabilitation Project Force," the
prison or concentration camp of Scientology. Being sent
to the RPF is the dread of every Sea Org member.

It was conceived by Hubbard during one of his low
points, at a time when he was recovering from a
motorcycle accident and in a generally black mood:

It was not until early 1974
that blatant breaking of another
person's will—"break 'em down,

---

[127] Tonja Burden affidavit

build 'em back up"—became full
blown and implemented as
official dogma: the Rehabilitation
Project Force.

The RPF was essentially a
slave-labor prison project, where
inmates ate scraps from the table
after other crew had finished,
and where they were not allowed
to speak to any nonRPFers
unless spoken to. Even then,
they were only to briefly answer,
while addressing their betters as
"Sir." RPFers were dressed in
blue overalls and had to run
wherever they went. (I shouldn't
be describing this in past tense.
The RPF continues to this day,
very much a part of the Church
of Scientology.)[128]

Gerry Armstrong was a graduate of the RPF, and he
writes:

There is no way to really
describe the RPF experience, the
hopelessness, the humiliation,
the horror. It seemed to go on
forever, the days all identical, no
time to oneself, the same blue
boiler suits like prison garb, day
after day, the same questions in
the same endless security
checks.

Hubbard's purpose in
creating the RPF, and running it
as a prison with assignees

---

[128] Corydon, p. 95

considered criminals, was the
breaking of people's wills, the
total subjugation of anyone he
considered exhibited "counter-
intention" to his goals.

He achieved his purpose
with me so well that I thanked
him for the opportunity of doing
the RPF, much like prisoners of
war, who are broken emotionally
and spiritually, through
deprivation and mind-control
techniques, and thank their
captors.[129]

Some of the rules in the RPF, as given by one person
who was in it, are:

1. No walking. You had to run all the time.
2. You weren't allowed to speak to anyone outside the
   RPF.
3. You weren't allowed to originate any
   communication to anyone outside the RPF unless
   there was an emergency.
4. You weren't allowed to go anywhere by yourself
   unless authorized to do so. Even when going to the
   bathroom, someone had to go with you.
5. You had to call all RPF seniors, "Sir." If there was
   some reason you had to talk to someone outside
   the RPF, you had to call him, "Sir."
6. All letters you wrote had to be put in a stamped,
   unsealed envelope, then dropped in a box in the
   RPF room. The RPF Ethics Officer read all outgoing
   mail.
7. You're allowed only in RPF-designated areas. You
   weren't allowed to go anywhere else except during

---

[129] Ibid, p. 98

morning cleaning stations when you cleaned the rest of the (org).

8. You had to wear dark-blue boiler suits or dark-blue shirts and pants.
9. You weren't allowed "luxuries," such as music, watching TV, playing cards, perfume, radios, etc.

This same member talks about his/her state of mind while being audited in the RPF:

> My Rock Slam handling (a type of auditing) I think was the point where my brain wasn't just falling apart but it started to get fried. I was running out all of these evil purposes connected to the Rock Slams (a certain needle read on the E-meter), and I started spouting out and running out the weirdest things, like, "to be somebody else," "to blow up a planet," "commit suicide," "to never grow up," "to kill myself," "to destroy bodies." The list was endless.
>
> My brain was just getting fried on all of this. I mean, I had to have been the most evil and craziest person that ever existed. I don't know how to describe what happened other than my brain was frying right up. I felt like I was in a daze half the time. I'd do things, sort of like watching myself doing them but not realizing I was doing it, as if it was somebody else, except that I know it was me.
>
> I'd scream at my auditor. I'd throw down the cans to the E-

meter that I was holding. I'd
refuse to get auditing. I just
created a scene. So of course, I
ended up in Ethics and had a
"bodyguard" put on me.

This whole thing was a
period of weeks, I think. But
actually, in the state I was in, it
could have been two days or it
could have been two
months....[130]

Fortunately, this member was also able to escape and
is no longer in Scientology.

Another ex-member describes the process of mind
control in the RPF, in which the will is gradually eroded
and finally snaps:

Blind obedience violated
everything I had ever valued. I
had thought that Scientology was
about independence and self-
determinism, not blind obedience
to authority, or so Hubbard told
us on his many tapes I had
listened to when I was a student.

The RPF went against
everything I had imagined
Scientology to be, and I couldn't
even begin to reconcile the
contradiction. Here I was, a
prisoner, and what had I been
guilty of? I felt that there must be
something very wrong with me to
have gotten into such a mess.

I went through one

---

[130] Affidavit of an unnamed (by choice) ex-member of Scientology

hopeless day after another,
cleaning the toilets, drenched in
sweat and chlorine, and at night
trying to get something
accomplished in my auditing
program, always to no avail.

One day, a Sea Org officer
remarked to me that I was not
even worth the $5 (RPFers only
got half pay), and I agreed.

I started to feel like my
sanity was slipping away, what
little there was of it. I can
remember one day walking down
the stairs to Lower Hold Number
One and getting a sensation like I
was going to totally disappear—
like I was going to experience a
complete spiritual death. It's very
difficult to describe. I felt like I
was going to be completely
annihilated.

One day I completely broke
down. I went down into the lower
hold where the RPF classroom
was and sobbed uncontrollably. I
cried like I had never cried
before. It felt like I was never
going to stop.

Later, when I finally
managed to stop, I went above
decks and just sat, looking out at
the water. I thought about how
much of my identity had been
tied up in being a good auditor. I
felt like I was nothing if I couldn't
produce as a Scientologist. I just
sat there and gazed out at the

sea.

The next day, my grief came back. I went through several days where I couldn't stop crying. I can remember one day scrubbing the floor of one of the bathrooms as hard as I could, but no amount of scrubbing could cleanse me. I felt as if I were being raped. I was in a deep state of mourning for a loss I couldn't define.

Sometimes, a person's emotions are way ahead of what can be thought or verbalized. This was the case with me at the time; my feelings were giving me signals, but I was unable to listen to them. In retrospect, I came to realize that on an emotional level, I knew that Scientology was a sham. I had no words to describe my loss at the time, and there was no one to help me see what was happening. All I knew was that I felt worse than I had ever felt in my life.

What I really needed was someone to jump start my mind so I could start thinking again and get in touch with what my feelings were trying to tell me, which was, "Scientology is a sham. Get out of here, now! You have been lied to and are now in a trap. This is what you gave up your education, your family, and your friends for. The illusion is shattered. Now there is nothing left for you here in Scientology."

It was the biggest loss I had ever experienced in my life—a loss of my innocence, a loss of trust, and a loss of a dream that I thought had become a reality.

So I continued on in the RPF, doing my labor and in tears most of the time.

I made one final attempt to assert myself. One day I was standing watch as Quartermaster, logging people on and off the ship. This was a duty that RPFers were often assigned to do. One day, I had been on watch all morning, and someone was supposed to relieve me so I could have lunch, but no one showed up. Finally, I went below decks to the aft lounge to see what happened to my relief person.

A Sea Org officer was having lunch with some other RPFers, and he refused to help me. I just exploded. My anger had very little to do with what was actually going on—I just felt I had to make one last attempt to assert myself.

I said, "To hell with all of you. I'm going to have my lunch!" at which point, the Sea Org officer said, "That's it. You're assigned to the RPF's RPF."

And so it came to pass that

I was assigned to the RPF's RPF. I spent very long days down in the engine room, cleaning foul-smelling muck out of the bilges and then painting them. I was assigned a Condition of Enemy, and to get out of it, I had to write up the formula, which was, *Find out who you really are.*

I wrote up the formula and submitted it to the Ethics Officer, but he wouldn't accept what I had written. I didn't know what he wanted me to write.

For days, I struggled to find the answer, as I was cleaning the bilges. At that point, I really didn't know. If I had known who I really was, I would have let them throw me out and gotten as far away from the ship and everyone aboard as I could.

Years later, when I read Lifton's studies of the Communist Chinese, I realized that my struggle to write up the Condition of Enemy formula was very much like the struggle the prisoners must have gone through to write up confessions that were "sincere" enough to satisfy their captors.

In both cases, it wasn't enough just to physically imprison the person. The person had to agree to and participate in their mental imprisonment as well, and, if the statements written up weren't deemed as sincere, the person had to rewrite the statement until it satisfied the people in charge.

The Ethics Officers kept rejecting my formula. This went on for days, which I spent down in the engine room. I wasn't allowed to communicate with anyone except for the Ethics Officer. Even if someone spoke to me, I wasn't allowed to respond.

One day, another Sea Org member broke the rules and spoke to me. I dutifully told him that he wasn't allowed to speak to me, nor I to him, but he told me not to worry about it. I'll never forget what he did for me that day, just by breaking the rules and talking to me. I don't exactly recall what he said, but he encouraged me to hang in there and helped me feel I could make it through this horrendous experience. He showed me compassion when I needed it the most.

I determined that I would hang onto what little sanity I had left. The way I did this was to shut off all my emotions. It was a matter of survival.

The next day, I finally wrote up my formula to the Ethics Officer's satisfaction and got out of the RPF's RPF. I had been broken after a long, hard struggle.

I was no longer angry. I
was no longer sad. I was no
longer happy. I felt nothing. I
simply did as I was told.

At long last, I had learned
the lesson of the RPF.[131]

It is fact that whenever someone becomes psychotic
in Scientology, and this does happen with not surprising
regularity, the person is assigned to the RPF for
"rehabilitation." The inhumane treatment of the mentally
ill in Scientology is a matter that has never been
addressed by any agency outside Scientology. This
inhumanity is graphically described by a "survivor of
Scientology" who writes about her last days in the
organization:

My last week in the Sea
Org was like a dream. One night,
I was told to go to the basement
and stuff letters. I did this in a
little room with no ventilation
and moisture dripping down the
walls.

There was never anyone
around. I was left alone most of
the time at night now. That was
their mistake. It gave me time to
think.

This night, I started
stuffing my 2,000 letters. The
old, innocent days of the Sea Org
seemed very far away. The
idealistic little girl who had come
here in '74 with dreams of
newfound powers and increased

---

[131] Excerpt from *My Nine Lives in Scientology* by Monica Pignotti

understanding had died....

Far above me, the Org hummed with activity. Every day, someone else like me, gullible and hungry for answers, was being drawn into Scientology. Every day, someone joined the Sea Org looking for security within the group, not knowing the total control of their personality they were handing over. Every day, someone was sent to the RPF. These were my thoughts as I stood there.

Suddenly, I flung the letters down. I needed to walk. Underneath the nine buildings were long tunnels that connected each building. Great steam pipes ran along the sides of the tunnels. It was like being in the engine room of a ship. The public didn't know that these tunnels existed.

I walked for miles, thinking.

I knew now that I was going to die. My body was completely emaciated. My mind had developed frightening blank periods when I could remember nothing at all. I had very few emotions I could feel anymore. Things were breaking down.

I walked through tunnels I had never been in. Then I heard it—inhuman screaming and ranting. It was coming from my right.

There were four doors, and someone was pounding on one of them. I ran over and tried to open the door. It was locked. I yelled, "Are you all right?" I got more screams.

Suddenly, someone touched my shoulder. I turned and looked at a man in clean overalls.

"Hello," he said. "I'm the Ethics Officer for the RPF."

"What are you doing to her?" I asked.

"Oh, she's just blowing off some charge. When someone flips out on the RPF, we lock them up for a couple of hours. They calm down after a while." He smiled.

I was stunned. "You lock them up in here?"

"Sure. You know the tech. The tech always works."

I looked at him, totally triumphant, with Scientology tech on his side. I felt sick to my stomach. The corridor started spinning around me.

So this was it—the final answer, cold, calculated, step-by-step—a progression to stamp out anyone who questioned, rebelled, criticized, disliked Scientology. Break them, all of us. You don't agree, you make a mistake, you

are a staff member, and you flip
out. No mercy, just Scientology
tech. Pure Ron Hubbard, turned
insane.

He was still looking at me.

"Sure," I said. "Maybe she'll
drop her body and pick up a new
one. She'll get regged again and
come back for another try. Death
doesn't exist, does it? Suffering
doesn't exist, either, only the
tech sent from another galaxy."

"Wow," he said. "What OT
level are you?"

"None you'd want to know
about."
I turned and left him standing by
the locked door.[132]

The purpose of the Sea Organization, according to the
Dianetics and Scientology *Technical Dictionary,* is to "get
ethics in on the planet and eventually the universe."

The possibility is truly frightening.

---

[132] Corydon, p. 130

CHAPTER TEN

Religion, Incorporated—The Selling of Scientology

Scientology 1970 is being planned on a religious-organization basis throughout the world.

This will not upset in any way the usual activities of the organization. It is entirely a matter for accountants and solicitors.

Religion by L. Ron Hubbard

I entreat you students not to be carried away by the claims that any and many "teachers" or "masters" make. ESPECIALLY, BEWARE OF ANY TEACHER, OR SCHOOL, WHICH CLAIMS TO HAVE ABSOLUTE TRUTH AND ESPECIALLY WATCH YOUR MONEY DONATIONS.

The Art and Practice of the Occult, by Ophiel

During the 1930s, L. Ron Hubbard had acquired a formidable reputation as a writer of pulp fiction and science fiction. Fans looked forward to his swashbuckling tales each month, and they were rarely disappointed. Whether it was westerns, full of the drama and dust of the West, or adventures set in the exotic Orient, or eerie science-fiction tales, Hubbard seemed to have tapped into an inexhaustible supply of plots and characters. His fertile imagination, coupled with a prodigious writing talent, his capacity for amazingly prolific verbal output, made him the envy of many of his fiction-writing peers.

Any lesser man would've been satisfied with the success that Hubbard found as an adventure writer, but Hubbard was no ordinary man. Burning inside him was, as he once confided to an associate, "an insatiable lust for money and power." More than once, he remarked to friends that he was considering starting his own religion. He told one friend that he had not decided whether to destroy the Catholic Church or "merely start a new one."[133]

He also made the now-famous quote at a writer's conference that it was silly to write for a penny a word, and that the real way to make a million dollars was to start your own religion.

Scientology is about money. In *Governing Policy,* Hubbard wrote:

> MAKE MONEY. MAKE
> MONEY. MAKE MORE MONEY.
> MAKE OTHER PEOPLE
> PRODUCE SO AS TO MAKE
> MONEY.

Hubbard was probably one of the, if not the, most successful con men who ever lived. He was able to convince thousands of people to sell their homes, liquidate their assets, and give everything they had to him in exchange for the questionable commodity of spiritual salvation for eternal lifetimes to come. Not only did they buy it, they bought it fully believing they'd made the best of the bargain.

---

[133] Miller, p. 144

A recent issue of *Impact,* the Scientology magazine, contains a revealing list of "Patrons of the Association," 972 people who have donated money to the International Association of Scientologists. What is remarkable about this list is that of the 972 donors listed, 844 donated more than $40,000, 99 donated more than $100,000, and 29 donated over $250,000—for a grand total of over $50 million!

That kind of giving by parishioners might well be the envy of other churches.

It has always been difficult for outsiders to ascertain certain information about Scientology, because of the organization's secrecy related to financial and membership statistics and the tendency of the organization to inflate or deflate those numbers to their advantage.

As far back as 1978, Scientology claimed to have 5,437,000 members internationally. For the past ten years, they have claimed to have six million members globally, yet, in an internal church memo released this year, Scientologists were told that the membership of the church was 25,000, and they were exhorted to work to increase that figure by a factor of four so that the church would have 100,000 members.

Conversely, the church has systematically underreported its income and assets. Reports from defecting members have, however, provided some clues to Scientology's finances.

In the September, 1981, issue of *Reader's Digest* was a report that at that time, Scientology was grossing $100 million a year, a figure substantiated by courtroom testimony one year later, in which a recent defector from Scientology reported that the church was grossing $2 million a week. It was also reported that the church in Clearwater alone was grossing $1 million a week, and that the staff was put on a diet of rice and beans when that quota wasn't met.

The same court testimony produced the information that at least $100 million had been illegally smuggled from the US and stashed in various foreign accounts in Liechtenstein and Luxembourg. *Forbes Magazine* in 1986 reported that the net worth of the church at that time was $400 million.

Scientologists, especially those working as "staff," are constantly pressured to increase the flow of funds into the organization. An example of that is what one writer dubbed *the billion-dollar caper.*

In a taped briefing to his staff, Hubbard said, "Money! Repeat money! Repeat money! Repeat money!"[134]

Scientology always had a network of "missions," small Scientology organizations accessible to the public that offered beginning Scientology services. The owners of those missions were probably the only entrepreneurs in Scientology, and many did very well financially.

Until 1982, those missions were loosely organized by the Scientology Missions Office World Wide. In 1982, Scientology, under its new leadership, and presumably masterminded by Hubbard, decided to "nationalize" those missions and milk the affluent owners of their assets.

It was announced to those mission holders that a new umbrella organization was being established—the Scientology Missions International. Many of the mission holders were required to buy a $35,000 "mission starters packet," even though their missions had been operating for years.

To add insult to injury, the mission holders were informed that their missions were to be visited by the International Finance Police, who would go over their finances—a privilege for which the mission would pay $15,000 per day. The International Finance Police were organized by an International Finance Dictator.

---

[134] Corydon, p. 200

Through those and other terrorist acts, a full-scale purge took place, in which many long-standing Scientologists were thrown or forced out of the organization by the new management—the children who grew up under Hubbard—who ruthlessly seized power.

"I have never lied to you," Hubbard once assured his followers.

Yet, in an article entitled *What Your Donations Buy,* he wrote:

> I know that Dianetics and Scientology services should be free, and I wish they were.
>
> Personally, I have tried to do my part in this. None of the researches of Dianetics and Scientology were ever actually paid for out of organizational fees. With the typewriter, I paid for the research myself.
>
> Independent of church costs, the 13 ½ million dollars that churches owed me for services rendered, the usual author's royalties, lectures, loans, and things paid out of my own pocket, I forgave and never collected.
>
> So the donations you make for services do not go to me....

Hubbard then claimed that the money from Scientology was spent in "keeping the church alive and functioning and the environment safe."

So where did Hubbard get his money?

In the 60s, Hubbard told a reporter from *The Daily Mail* in England that he had $7 million in a Swiss bank, money, he claimed, that he inherited in oil land in Montana.

Defectors from Scientology in the 80s portray a different picture. According to the *Forbes Magazine* issue of October 27, 1986, in 1982, at least $40 million went directly to Hubbard, channeled through various Scientology corporations.

One defector, Homer Schomer, said that in 1983, he personally made out checks to Hubbard each week for $1 million from Scientology funds. In other words, Hubbard was making $52 million a year from Scientology. A dozen different corporations were set up to disguise those payments to Hubbard.

According to one ex-member:

> The problem was, how were we going to get the money to Hubbard? He was not supposed to take the money personally. So separate corporations were set up. This is RRF, Religious Research Foundation. We used to call it Ralph. That was a code name.
>
> Money would be put into Ralph, that would be accounts in Liechtenstein. This is a Liberian Corporation, and he would draw money from it. So in other words, all of this money actually made its way over to Ralph. It went through these various people and various organizations, and from Ralph, then it went right to Hubbard.[135]

---

[135] Ibid, p. 199

Later a simpler means of channeling money to Hubbard was devised, which was for Hubbard to bill Scientology retroactively for his various services and research. For example, Hubbard billed the church $85 million for the use of the E-meter, which he claimed to have developed.

If not already obvious, the mercenary nature of Scientology can be clearly seen in many of its policies and practices.

One example is a policy Hubbard called *How to Sell Scientology,* an interesting title for the policy of a church. In that policy, he instructed his followers to talk about the brutality of psychiatry, saying, *If you get real insistent, even oddly accusative of the listener, even slightly angry on this point and stress it over and over, you should get some people willing to come to a (lecture).*

Another bulletin announced the *Overwhelming Public Popularity* campaign, in which a media blitz in the San Francisco area would *get the broad, general public knowing about and wanting Scientology.*

How many churches have a trained corps of salespersons working on a commission basis to provide a constant supply of paying public to the organization? How many churches offer rebates on the services purchased by parishioners?

In Scientology, salespersons, called FSMs (Field Staff Members), are trained to recruit people for Scientology services. The FSMs earn 10-15% commission on everyone they select for a Scientology service, depending on the type of service.

FSMs are drilled on the "dissemination drill," in which they learn to locate a person's ruin. The drill has four steps—1. contact; 2. handle; 3. salvage; and 4. bring to understanding.

The FSM contacts a potential recruit in various ways, "handles" any objections he might have about

Scientology, then probes through conversation to discover the person's "ruin," the one thing in his life he'd pay almost anything to overcome. Once that is discovered, the person can be "brought to understanding" by being told, "Scientology handles that (problem)."

Once the new person is on the Communication Course, he will be shepherded to subsequent courses by the FSM, who receive commissions for everything his selectee does in Scientology.

FSMs go through an intensive training course, in which they are given tips on how to increase their commissions. They're trained to use "Come-on" dissemination, in which they learn to create some mystery to attract the new person into Scientology. They're taught to use books, primarily the Dianetics book, to lure people into Scientology. They learn a technique called the "casualty contact," in which they go as "ministers" to hospitals to recruit people into Scientology.

FSMs are taught that their purpose is to "help LRH (Hubbard), contact, handle, salvage, and bring to understanding the individuals and thus the peoples of earth."[136]

For successful FSMs, there's even the FSM of the Year Award, at which the FSM with the highest statistics for the year receives a silver cup.

When a new person begins a course in Scientology, he's told that if he doesn't like the course, he can have a full refund. What he isn't told is the lengths to which he has to go to obtain the promised refund. A dissatisfied person applying for a refund in Scientology is first subjected to an extensive routing form, requiring him to go around the organization and be interviewed by at least twelve people about the reason he wants a refund. Even after completing that tortuous procedure, there's not a

---

[136] Hubbard policy of 9 May 1965, *Field Auditors Become Staff*

guarantee he'll ever receive his refund. He may find that his letters and repeated phone calls go unanswered indefinitely, until he finally needs the services of an attorney to recover the promised refund.

Another Scientology policy is the "freeloader's bill." A person who signs on as "staff" in a Scientology organization by signing either a 2 ½ year, 5 year, or billion-year contract of employment is technically entitled to free services, auditing or training. However, if the person becomes dissatisfied and decides to leave staff, he is immediately given a freeloader's bill, in which he's billed for all services he received as a staff member—at full rates.

Since the charges for auditing run from $300-$1,000 per hour, that bill can be very intimidating to a staff person, particularly when he is threatened with expulsion from Scientology or a "lower condition" unless he pays. Since most Scientologists believe that their spiritual survival for the "next endless trillions of years" depend on Scientology, the threat of being expelled or having his relationship with Scientology jeopardized is no small matter.

There's an even more ominous policy in Scientology, having to do with defectors from the organization. The person in Scientology undergoing auditing is continually told that his auditing file is confidential. That's done so he feels comfortable divulging even his most personal thoughts to the auditor. Unbeknownst to the person being audited, the organization has a policy called GO Order 121669, which orders the culling of confessional folders for information to use against people who are "security leaks."

In one such case, a Scientologist wrote a letter to someone who was obviously dissatisfied, explaining, *The review (of his folder) shows that you actually make more money than you report to the IRS, and that you are skimming around $2,500 off the top prior to reports.* The author threatened to make that information public if the person didn't get back in line.

One judge who looked into Scientology called it, "The world's largest organization of unqualified persons engaged in the practice of dangerous techniques which masquerade as mental therapy."[137]

Is Scientology a religion, or is it a business masquerading as a religion? The reader must judge for himself.

---

[137] Justice Andersen, Supreme Court of Victoria, Australia

CHAPTER ELEVEN

Ethics—The Greatest Good for the Greatest Number of Dynamics?

Hubbard does not bother to justify the inhumanity of his Ethics.If families are broken up, if friends are turned against friends, if suicides occur, if an entrapment of the very spirit that makes humans human should occur, then that is subsidiary to the aim to prove Hubbard right. After all, as he is careful to instill into the outlook of his followers, anything that happens to anyone is fully and totally that person's own responsibility, they pull it in on themselves, don't they?

The Mindbenders by Cyril Vosper

RC-45: An enormously effective process for exteriorization but its use is frowned upon by this society at this time.

Scientology's execution procedure, from *Creation of Human Ability,* by L. Ron Hubbard

The systems of thought and mind control devised by Hubbard in Scientology were very good—but not perfect. As in all organizations, there would inevitably be a few troublesome souls who would question, doubt, and generally resist the program. It was to deal with this troublesome remnant that Hubbard developed his system of *ethics,* which would effectively close the loop of Scientology's social control.

Like being sent to the principal's office in grade school, the order, "Go to ethics," strikes a certain terror in a Scientologist's soul. That's because the Ethics Officer holds the ultimate power in Scientology—to apply the dreaded label of "Suppressive Person" and to cast a member from Scientology, into spiritual oblivion for millions of lifetimes to come. A Scientologist will do almost anything to stay out of trouble with Ethics.

"Ethics" is defined by Scientology as rationality toward the highest level of survival among the dynamics. In Scientology, ethics has to do primarily with the group, which is Scientology. Anything that promotes or benefits Scientology is therefore defined as ethical, whereas anything that is contrasurvival for Scientology becomes, by definition, unethical.

Similarly, there is a phrase frequently heard in Scientology, "The greatest good for the greatest number of dynamics." It means that whatever is good for the group (Scientology) and for mankind is more important and takes precedence over whatever is good for the individual—a dangerous philosophy.

The chart of "ethics conditions" in Scientology is, in descending sequence:

Power
Power Change
Affluence
Normal Operation
Emergency
Danger

Nonexistence
Liability
Doubt
Enemy
Treason
Confusion

The theory in Scientology is that a person will always be in one of those conditions regarding any area of his life. One could be in a condition of Affluence on his job, Emergency in his marriage, Nonexistence in his finances, and Normal Operation regarding his health.

For each condition, Hubbard devised a formula, which, if applied, was supposed to cause the person to progress to the next-higher condition. That some of the formulas might not make sense doesn't matter, because Ron said that was what they are, so they must be right.

The formula for the condition of Confusion is, *Find out where you are.*

Once that was done, the person moved up to Treason, where the formula is, *Find out that you are.*

In Enemy, the formula is, *Find out who you really are.*

The formula for Doubt is a bit more complex. When one can't make up his mind concerning an individual, group, organization, or project, a condition of Doubt exists. The formula is:

1. Inform oneself honestly of the actual intentions and activities of that individual, group, project, or organization, brushing aside all bias and rumor.
2. Examine the statistics of the individual, group, project or organization.
3. Decide on the basis of

"The greatest good for the greatest number of dynamics" whether or not it should be attacked, harmed, suppressed, or helped.

4. Evaluate oneself or one's own group, project, or organization as to intentions and objectives.

5. Evaluate one's own or one's group, project, or organization's statistics.

6. Join or remain in or befriend the one which progresses toward the greatest good for the greatest number of dynamics and announce the fact publicly to both sides.

7. Do everything possible to improve the actions or statistics of the person, group, project, or organization one has remained in or joined.

8. Suffer on up through the conditions of the new group if one has changed sides, or the conditions of the group one has remained in if wavering from it has lowered one's status.

Once upgraded by the Ethics Officer to the condition of Liability, the formula is:

1. Decide who are one's friends.

2. Deliver an effective blow to the enemies of the group one has been pretending to be part of despite personal danger.

3. Make up the damage one has done by personal contribution far beyond the ordinary demands of a group member.

4. Apply for reentry to the group by asking the permission of each member of it to rejoin and rejoining only by majority permission, and, if refused, repeating steps 2-4 until one is allowed to be a group member again.

When a person first begins a job in Scientology, he starts off in a condition of Nonexistence, for which the formula is:

1. Find a comm (communication) line

2. Make yourself known

3. Discover what is needed and wanted

4. Do, produce, and/or present it

In other words, find out what needs to be done and do it. Having done that, one is now in a condition of Danger. That condition applies when an activity is in trouble. The formula is:

1. Bypass (ignore the junior in charge of the activity and handle it personally)
2. Handle the situation and any danger in it
3. Assign the area where it had to be handled a danger condition
4. Handle the personnel by ethics investigation
5. Reorganize the activity so that the situation will not repeat
6. Recommend any firm policy that will hereafter detect and/or prevent the condition from recurring

When the person has gotten his activity out of danger, he or she is then in a condition of Emergency, for which the formula is:

1. Promote and produce
2. Change your operating basis
3. Economize
4. Then prepare to deliver
5. Stiffen discipline or stiffen ethics

If the person has successfully applied the Emergency formula, the condition of Normal Operations now applies, and its formula is:

1. Don't change anything
2. Ethics are mild
3. If a statistic betters, look it over carefully and find out what bettered it and

> then do that without
> abandoning what you
> were doing before

4. Every time a statistic
   worsens slightly, quickly
   find out why and remedy
   it

If things are going well, and the formula for Normal Operation has been applied for a period of time, then the person could be said to be in a condition of Affluence, for which the formula is:

1. Economize. Be sure you
   don't buy anything with a
   future commitment to it

2. Pay every bill

3. Invest the remainder in
   service facilities, make it
   more possible to deliver

4. Discover what caused the
   condition of affluence and
   strengthen it

If things are going really well, the person may make a Power Change into another area of endeavor. If not, the person is in a condition of Power for which the only rule is: Don't disconnect—take ownership and responsibility for your connections.

These are the Ethics Conditions in Scientology, and they're taken very seriously. Each week, each person working for the organization, i.e., on staff, turns in his "stats" to the Ethics Officer. He is assigned a condition by the Ethics Officer and required to apply the appropriate formula for that condition to his job. In addition, the Ethics Officer can assign a person a condition in any area of his personal life, and the person must apply the appropriate formula and submit a written application to the Ethics Officer before upgrading to the next-higher condition. For a Scientologist, ethics conditions and their formulas are a way of life.

Another function of ethics in Scientology is the administration of "security checks" to members. Security checks, or sec checks, are administered with the member on the E-meter. In this case, the E-meter is used as a lie detector.

The first sec check encountered by a member will be the Staff Questionnaire, which is given when that person first joins staff. Some of the items on the questionnaire are:

1.   Name
2.   Life history
3.   How did you come into Scientology?
4.   History in Scientology
5.   Do you have any psychiatric-institutional history?
6.   Do you have a criminal record?
7.   Do you have any crimes for which you could be arrested?
8.   Do you have any physical disabilities or illnesses?
9.   Do you have any record of insanity?
10. Are you connected to anyone who is antagonistic to Scientology or spiritual healing?
11. Have any of your family members threatened to

sue or attack or
embarrass Scientology?

12. What are the details of
your 2D (second dynamic,
or love life) history over
the last year, with names
and dates?

13. Have you any homosexual
or lesbian history—when
and with whom?

14. Drug history

15. Are you here for any
different purpose than
you say?

Sec checks are a fact of life in Scientology. It must be remembered that should a member defect, his ethics folder with the written answers to those questions can be used, per Guardian's Order 121669, to blackmail or otherwise intimidate the defector.

One of the earliest sec checks was called the Joburg. It was developed in Johannesburg, South Africa, and was a much feared security check for many years. Sample questions from that interrogation include the following:

Have you ever stolen anything?
Have you ever been in prison?
Have you ever embezzled money?
Have you ever been in jail?
Have you ever had anything to do with
pornography?
Have you ever been a drug addict?
Do you have a police record?
Have you ever raped anyone?
Have you ever been involved in an abortion?
Have you ever committed adultery?
Have you ever practiced homosexuality?
Have you ever had intercourse with a member of
your family?

Have you ever slept with a member of a race of another color?
Have you ever bombed anything?
Have you ever murdered anyone?
Have you ever been a Communist?
Have you ever been a newspaper reporter?
Have you ever ill-treated children?
Have you ever had anything to do with a baby farm?
Are you afraid of the police?
Have you ever done anything your mother would be ashamed to find out?
How do you feel about sex?
How do you feel about being controlled?

Later, the contents of this security check were revised into *The Only Valid Security Check,* which contains many of the same questions and has several others added, such as:

Have you ever practiced cannibalism?
Have you ever peddled dope?
Have you practiced sex with animals?
Have you ever attempted suicide?
Do you collect sexual objects?
Have you ever practiced sex with children?
Have you ever practiced masturbation?
Have you ever killed or crippled animals for pleasure?
Have you ever had unkind thoughts about L. Ron Hubbard?
Are you upset about this security check?

As if that weren't enough, there is the lengthy *Whole Track Sec Check,* designed to ferret out "overts" a person has committed during his thousands of past lives. Of the 346 questions on that form, a few are:

Have you ever enslaved a population?
Have you ever sacked a city?
Have you ever raped a child of either sex?

Have you ever bred bodies for degrading purposes?
Have you ever deliberately tortured someone?
Have you driven anyone insane?
Did you come to Earth for evil purposes?
Have you ever made a planet or nation radioactive?
Have you ever maimed or crippled other people's bodies?
Have you ever torn out someone's tongue?
Have you ever blinded anyone?
Have you ever punished another by cutting off some
part of his body?
Have you ever smothered a baby?
Have you ever had sexual relations with an animal or a
bird?
Have you ever castrated anyone?
Have you ever applied a hot iron to another person's
body?
Have you ever beaten a child to death?
Have you ever eaten a human body?

There is even a special security check for children from the ages of six to twelve, who are asked questions like:

What has somebody told you not to tell?
Have you ever decided you didn't like some member
of your family?
Have you ever pretended to be sick?
Have you ever bullied a smaller child?
Have you ever been mean to an animal, bird, or
fish?
Have you ever broken something belonging to
someone else?
Have you ever done anything you were very much
ashamed of?
Have you ever failed to finish your schoolwork on
time?
Have you ever lied to a teacher?
Have you ever done anything to someone else's
body that you shouldn't have?
Have you ever been ashamed of your parents?

Have you ever lied to escape blame?
Have you ever told stories about someone behind
his back?

Similar to security checks is another assignment
frequently meted out by the Ethics Officer, and that is to
write up one's OWs, overts and withholds, which, in
Scientology, means all the things one has ever done
wrong (overts) and especially those that someone else
almost found out about (withholds).

That will commonly be assigned to a person who is in
the process of "working out of a condition of Enemy." The
Ethics Officer is usually not satisfied until many pages of
OWs have been produced by the properly repentant
member.

At one point in Scientology, it was the practice to lock
a member in a closet for two or more days while he wrote
up his sins.

If a person in Scientology should become querulous,
especially if he found fault with something Hubbard wrote
or showed doubt about a point of dogma, he would be
quickly isolated from other students and dispatched to
Ethics until his overts could be discovered and dealt with.

Anything written by Hubbard (Source) is assumed
valid and true. Therefore, anyone who disagrees with
anything he wrote must have personal overts that cause
him to find fault.

It's the job of the Ethics department of Scientology to
assign the person the appropriate lower condition and
have him write up his OWs until he sees the light and can
be returned a more obedient, humble member of the
group.

In the case of serious deviation from the group norm,
there are more severe penalties that can be applied to
provide the motivation for a member to conform. Some of
those penalties in the past included:

A dirty gray rag tied to the left arm to indicate a condition of liability.

Confinement to the premises of the organization.

Suspension of pay and dismissal from post.

A black mark on the left cheek to indicate a condition of treason.

The person can't be communicated with by anyone in the organization.

Deprivation of sleep for up to 72 hours.

Assignment of manual labor for up to 72 hours.

In the case of persons who become actual enemies of the organization, the Ethics order of Fair Game can be applied, which means that such persons may be "deprived of property or injured by any means by any Scientologist without any discipline of the Scientologist. May be tricked, sued, lied to, or destroyed."

At one time, Hubbard ordered the ultimate punishment for thirteen people who had defected as "enemies" from the organization. He ordered that "auditing process R2-45" be used on them if any Scientologist saw them.

R2-45 is a term that is understood by any Scientologist. When he first demonstrated it, it is said that Hubbard fired a Colt .45 revolver through the floor of the stage on which he lectured. Routine 2-45 refers to the act of shooting someone in the head with a Colt .45 and is the execution procedure in Scientology. In defending themselves, Scientologists say Hubbard was joking.

However, in a document entitled *Racket Exposed,* Hubbard did, in fact, order thirteen people shot on sight.

Other aspects of the system of social control enforced by the Ethics arm of the organization are Knowledge Reports and Committees of Evidence.

Knowledge Reports were introduced by Hubbard in 1965. It is similar to the system used in a Communist country, in which everyone spies on everyone else.

In Scientology, if you see someone doing something wrong, you must write up a Knowledge Report on that person to be sent to Ethics for *handling.* Hubbard justified that system in a policy letter entitled *Knowledge Reports,* in which he wrote:

> To live at all, one has to
> exert some control over his
> equals as well as his juniors and
> (believe it or not) his superiors.
>
> And get a REAL group in
> return that, collectively can
> control the environment and
> prosper, because its group
> members individually help
> control each other.

A person in the organization suspected of being a dreaded "suppressive person," will be called before the Scientology version of a jury trial, called a Committee of Evidence, or Comm Ev. A Comm Ev, however, has little to do with justice, as the results have frequently been determined ahead of time, and the Comm Ev itself is just a formality through which the offending person can be officially declared SP and ousted from the organization.

A Suppressive Person in Scientology is defined as one who "actively seeks to suppress or damage Scientology or a Scientologist by Suppressive Acts." A Suppressive is basically anyone who's an enemy of Scientology. It's hard to convey the terror that the words "suppressive person" arouse in a Scientologist. It means someone is thoroughly evil and beyond redemption, his soul doomed for eternity.

Even being around an SP can be bad for one's health, spiritual and otherwise, and a person connected to an SP is known as a PTS, or Potential Trouble Source.

When a person becomes ill or is doing badly for any reason, it's assumed he's connected to an SP. When a Scientologist becomes ill, an auditing action, such as an "S and D," Search and Discovery, might be ordered to discover the identity of the SP in the person's environment. Once the SP is located and disconnected from, according to Scientology theory, the person should recover. It's a strange brand of medicine.

It's always assumed that Scientology is good, and those who are against it are, by nature, evil. In an article entitled *Why Some Fight Scientology,* Hubbard wrote:

> Scientology had no enemies until the word was out that it worked. Criminals, Communists, perverted religionists alike swarmed to support a "new fraud," a "hoax," a brand new way of extorting money from and enslaving Man.
>
> And then in 1950, they found that the new sciences worked with, to them, deadly accuracy. And with a shudder of terror, they faced about and struck with every weapon possible. The press, the courts, shady women, insane inmates, politicians, tax bureaus, these and many more were used in a frantic effort to beat down what they had found to be honest, decent, and accurate.

The unthinkable thought in Scientology is that something said by Hubbard is wrong. Doubt in Scientology is a "lower condition" to be punished. Scientology is a group in which there's no room for individuality, only conformity. That extends to the act of thinking.

What was most frightening for most people about George Orwell's novel *1984,* was that the one sacrosanct territory belonging to a man—his thoughts—had been violated and invaded by the state. In the real world, we are only responsible for and have to fear the consequences of our actions, but in Orwell's world, a man had to fear the consequences of his thoughts, too. Most of us would have to agree that living in a world in which we could be punished not only for what we did but also for what we thought would be frightening, indeed.

Scientology comes very close to being that kind of world. As Hubbard once said, "The E-meter sees all, knows all, tells everything." With Scientology auditing, there is a constant invasion into the privacy of the members' thoughts.

In Scientology, the Road to Total Freedom, Hubbard has created a world frighteningly similar to the nightmarish world of Orwell's fantasy. In Scientology, the system of Ethics is Big Brother, constantly watching over all.

CHAPTER TWELVE

OSA (Office of Special Affairs)

The Secret CIA of Scientology

Remember one thing, we are not running a business, we are running a government. We are in direct control of people's lives.

L. Ron Hubbard Policy letter of 5 August, 1959

By the mid-1950s, Scientology was a religion under siege. In the US, the church had been raided by the FDA. In England, Scientology was being investigated by Parliament, and St. Hill students lived in danger of deportation. The Australian Inquiry was underway, and there were tremors in South Africa. Hubbard had been deported from Rhodesia and was under constant FBI surveillance at St. Hill.

Predisposed to paranoia, Hubbard wasn't one to remain on the defensive for long. *Don't ever defend, always attack,* he wrote. *If attacked on some vulnerable point by anyone or anything or any organization, always find or manufacture enough threats against them to cause them to sue for peace....*[138]

---

[138] Miller, p. 241

Evidence of the war mentality promoted by Hubbard and highly contagious within Scientology is a policy written by Hubbard entitled *The War,* in which he announced:

> You may not realize it...but
> there is only one small group
> that has hammered Dianetics
> and Scientology for eighteen
> years. The press attacks, the
> public upsets you receive...were
> generated by this one group. Last
> year we isolated a dozen men at
> the top. This year we found the
> organization these used and all
> its connections over the
> world....[139]

Hubbard claimed that a group of twelve men associated with the World Bank set up psychiatry and the mental health movement as a vehicle to undermine and destroy the West. That twelve-man conspiracy was the real source of all opposition to Scientology.

In February, 1966, Lord Balniel of the English House of Commons called for an investigation into Scientology. Hubbard responded by setting up the Public Investigation Section at St. Hill for the purposes of *helping LRH (Hubbard) investigate public matters and individuals which seem to impede human liberty,* and *to furnish intelligence.*[140]

By the late 60s, the Public Investigation Section had evolved into the Guardian's Office, a separate and unique agency within Scientology that became Hubbard's private intelligence bureau, a private CIA within the church.

---

[139] Ibid, p. 219

[140] Ibid, p. 254

Hubbard appointed his wife, Mary Sue, as Comptroller or head of the newly formed Guardian's Office, headquartered at St. Hill.

The Guardian's Office had six bureaus:

1. Legal, which handled litigation involving Scientology
2. Public Relations and media relations
3. Information, including the controversial Overt and Covert Data Collection and Operations Sections
4. Social Coordination, establishing the many Scientology "front organizations"
5. Service, for training GO staff members
6. Finance.

Branch One of the Information Bureau, called B-1, was the real nerve center of the GO, where files were maintained on all Scientologists, as well as on every perceived enemy of the organization.

Illegal and legal means of obtaining information were sanctioned. In a Scientology policy entitled *Re: Intelligence,* the following were given as possibilities for collecting data:

1. Infiltration
2. Bribery
3. Buying information
4. Robbery
5. Blackmail

In discussing the criminal policies of the Guardian's Office, it's important to remember the frame of reference from which Scientologists operate and from which these policies were conceived.

From a Scientology perspective, the world is in great danger of nuclear extinction, and Scientology exists as the only deterrent to that terrible inevitability.

To a Scientologist, Scientology is the elite organization on the planet, superior to all other earth organizations. The Scientology system of ethics, based on *the greatest good for the greatest number of dynamics,* is therefore superior to any system of wog law.

Transgressions of wog law necessary to further the ends of Scientology are sanctioned on the basis of the greatest good. In that way, lying, stealing, burgling, and a host of other crimes become justified as a means to the end of saving mankind.

Shielded by that philosophy, Scientologists have, over the years, been involved in a staggering array of crimes most unbecoming to members of a church.

It's a fact that Scientologists, particularly members of the GO, are trained to lie. In a policy entitled *Intelligence Specialist Training Routine—TR L (Training Routine Lie),* the student is trained *to outflow false data effectively.*

In the drill, the student has to tell a lie, which is then challenged by a coach, who works with the student until he becomes able to *lie facilely.*

The ability to lie convincingly is used by a Scientologist in a variety of situations, including giving courtroom testimony. A Scientologist feels no obligation to be truthful in a wog court, even under oath. Again, that's because he's operating under a higher law, that of *the greatest good for the greatest number of dynamics.*

Another Scientology policy contains a series of drills used to train GO agents. The student has to choose the best of several alternative solutions:

A. General scene: person to restrain/remove Mr.

Jones, employee in local government agency attacking the Org.

   1. Order hundreds of dollars' worth of liquor in Jones' name and have it delivered to his home to cause him trouble and make the liquor storeowner dislike him.

   2. Call up Jones' boss and accuse Jones of being a homosexual

   3. Send Jones' boss evidence of Jones accepting bribes on his job, with copies to the police and local FBI

B. General scene: a psychiatrist who has instigated attacks on the Org via police and press

   1. Expose his Nazi background to the press with evidence that he still attends local Nazi meetings

   2. Wake him up every night by calling him on the phone and threatening him

   3. Send a Field Staff Member in to be a patient of his for a year to disperse the psych during sessions

C. General Scene: a newspaper executive, Clyde McDonald, who's behind local attacks

   1. Poison him while he's asleep so he'll never start another attack

   2. Make known to the paper's owner that McDonald is responsible for the papers decreasing advertising revenues

   3. Spread a rumor around to the paper's employees that McDonald is a Communist

   4. Put itching powder in McDonald's clothes, so he'll scratch himself all day, thus preventing him from writing a story

   If those plans seem farfetched, an example of a Scientology operation actually carried out is the one against Paulette Cooper, who, in 1971, wrote a book critical of Scientology.

In church documents labeled *Operation PC (Paulette Cooper) Freakout* various scenarios were listed. In one, a Scientologist impersonating Cooper made threatening phone calls to the Arab consulate. Another plan was to mail a threatening letter to the same consulate, or make a bomb threat against it.

In still another plot, a Scientologist impersonating Cooper would go to a Laundromat and threaten to kill then-President Nixon or Henry Kissinger. Yet another plan was to get Paulette's fingerprints on a piece of paper, then type a bomb threat to Kissinger on the paper and mail it.

Something very similar to those was carried out. GO agents succeeded in getting Paulette's fingerprints on some stationery, then used it to make bomb threats against the church. Cooper was indicted on three counts of bomb threats and faced fifteen years in jail before she cleared herself by taking a sodium pentothal test.

Cooper was completely exonerated only when the FBI in their 1976 raid of the GO offices in Washington, DC, and Los Angeles, California, uncovered documents that detailed the church's plans to frame her.

Paulette Cooper's situation isn't unique. Many people who incurred the wrath of the Church of Scientology have found to what extent Scientologists will go in fighting "the enemy."

In one case, a woman found thousands of worms thrown at her front door. Defectors have been harassed by church agents spreading lies about them to employers or neighbors. Endless frivolous lawsuits have been launched. In one case, Boston attorney Michael Flynn narrowly avoided a crash when water was put in the gas tank of his plane. That occurred at a time when he represented several litigants against the church.

The FBI raids brought to light many of the written policies used to train GO members in criminal activities. One such policy is *Security and Theft of Materials*, which contains the following quotes:

> The first step in any breaking-and-entering job is casing. This consists of checking out the area to ascertain the possibilities for breaking into the premises....
>
> Professionals at all times wear gloves during an operation. This prevents fingerprints being left behind by which the agents could be traced....
>
> One trick used by professionals is...a series of cover stories are mocked up (invented) to cover each stage of the operation in the event that the operation is blown at any point.
>
> If you are picked up by the police, don't say anything more than you are required to by law, which is usually your name and address....

> Additionally, any agent working on such operations would have nothing in his possession that connected him with the organization (Scientology)....

That's an interesting policy letter for a church!

Another GO policy called *The Strike,* defines a strike as *the action of gathering information on a covert basis, performed by one or more agents.* An example of a strike actually carried out by the church was breaking into the IRS offices in Washington, DC, and photocopying all files related to Scientology.

A policy entitled *Walk-Ins* gives more detailed instructions for breaking and entering. Instructions are given for various aspects of burglarizing an office building—how to break into a locked Xerox machine, how to break into a locked door using a credit card, how to fashion a metal tool for breaking into a lock, how to use a strand of wire to break into a lock, how to break into a combination lock, etc. The policy comes complete with illustrations.

In a policy entitled *B&Es* (breaking and entering), the writer commented that *some of our most successful collections actions fall into this category.*

A good GO agent is also trained to bug and debug telephones in a policy entitled *Re: Debugging.* Also illustrated, that policy gives techniques for bugging and debugging phones, describes the four common types of bugs used, and explains the differences between a bug and a tap and how to deal with each.

Most Scientologists are unaware that their supposedly confidential auditing files are forwarded to the GO, where, should they defect from the organization, the folders will be systematically culled for information that can be used to intimidate or blackmail them.

Most Scientologists are unaware of GO policy #121669, entitled, *Programme: Intelligence: Internal Security,* which states:

Operating Targets: To make full use of all files of the organization to affect your major target. These include personnel files, Ethics files, training files, processing files, and requests for refunds....

The fact that a person's auditing or processing files may contain sensitive personal information given to an auditor under assurances of confidentiality is reflected in some of the reports generated by the GO from those folders.

In one such report, information gathered on a disaffected Scientologist included:

> While at the (Scientology
> org) she was promiscuous. She
> slept with four or five men during
> the course, two of them on the
> org premises. She has quite a
> record of promiscuity.... With
> three male preclears, she let
> them touch her genitals during
> sessions....
> She masturbated regularly
> since she was eight years old,
> mentions doing it once with
> coffee grounds and once had a
> puppy lick her....

Another such report includes the names of the person's children and the items:

Several self-induced abortions. Saw a psych due to alcoholism problems. Drug history: Librium, Valium, LSD, opium, heroin. Son is in jail, etc.

In 1973, Hubbard authored a plan for the GO called *Snow White,* instructing the GO to gain access to all federal agencies to obtain their files on Scientology. The name of the operation derived from Hubbard's opinion that once those agencies had their files "cleaned," Scientology would be "snow white."

Infiltrating, or penetrating, those agencies was achieved by having a Scientology agent obtain employment at an agency, then use his credentials to gain access to desired materials in the agency's files.

A report called *Compliance Report* lists 136 such agencies targeted for penetration, prioritized by a star system, with one star for low priority, two for higher, and three for highest. Some of the three-star agencies listed are the AEC, the CIA, the FBI, the FTC, the DFA, the IRS, the NSA, the US Air Force, the US Army, the US Attorney General, the DEA, the US Coast Guard, the US Department of Justice, the US Department of Labor, the US Department of State, the US Department of the Treasury, the US House of Representatives, the US Department of Immigration and Naturalization, the US Marshall's Office, the US Navy, the US Post Office, the US Selective Service, and the US Senate.

In that report, several agencies, such as the IRS, the DEA, the US Coast Guard, and the US Department of Labor were marked *Done.*

Another policy entitled *Safe* details plans to get agents into the US Attorney's offices in Washington, DC, and Los Angeles, into the IRS Office of International Operations, into the headquarters of the AMA, and into various state and local district attorneys' offices.

In a policy concerning the World Federation of Mental Health entitled *Compliance Report GO #121569*, the writer stated, *everything possible was done to collect the data, everything from infiltrating to stealing to eavesdropping, etc.*

The GO used a complex system of coding, especially in any written communications involving criminal or illegal activities. In policies such as *The Correct Use of*

Codes and *Re: Coding/Wording of Messages,* GO staff members are instructed to code the following:

> Incriminating, undercover activities and the like, such as violations of our status as a tax exempt nonprofit organization; subversive activities; covert operations; and money deals that might provoke government tax offices....

> Things that we want unknown as connected to the Church of Scientology, i.e., secret front groups;

> Words that would dispute the fact that the Church of Scientology's motives are humanitarian, i.e., harass, eradicate, attack, destroy, annihilate, entrapment....

> Admission to unpublished crimes and/or incriminating data;

> Mentions or the ordering of a B&E (breaking and entering);

> Implications of posing as a government agent;

> Evidence of tapping phone lines or illegal taping of conversations;

> Mentions of harassment;

> Any evidence of bribery;

> Wordings like, *Let's wipe him out;*

Another set of GO policies has to do with disposing of incriminating documents quickly should the org be raided by the FBI or other government agency.

One policy, known in the GO as *Red Box,* gives instructions for keeping all GO documents related to incriminating activities in a special folder or briefcase called the red box, which can be quickly destroyed in case of a raid.

Another policy, called *Basic and Essential Security,* instructs the GO staff member to be able to destroy all such incriminating material with 30-60 seconds. *Destruction by fire is usually most thorough and practical. Probably the easiest and least-expensive method is to purchase a metal container, some lighter fluid, and have matches on hand....*

Especially illuminating is the course check sheet for the *Information Full hat,* the course for training GO agents. Included on the course are:

To read a book on brainwashing;
To be able to define the following words: Spy, Spying, Agent, Operative, Information, Intelligence, Espionage, Counterespionage, counterintelligence, Fascism, Socialism, Communism, CIA, FBI, MI6, MI5, KGB, GRU
To write an essay on: What could happen if Intelligence was not anonymous or exclusive?
To read the following policy letters written by Hubbard:

Terror Stalks

Communism and Scientology

The War

PDH (Pain, Drugs, Hypnosis)

Intelligence

The Art of Building a Cover

Covert Operations I

Covert Operations II

Black PR

Secret, Notes on SMERSH

Etc.

Other books read on the course include The Spy and His Master; KGB; CIA and the Cult of Intelligence; Psychological Warfare against Nazi Germany; and The Art of War by Sun Tzu.

A sample of the hundreds of drills on this course:

Demo a covert operation on an opponent which restrains him and the beneficial result.

Demo why it is important to know your public's hate and love buttons when running an operation on an enemy.

Write an essay on what you would do if, while running operations on an opponent, the opponent begins to run a black propaganda campaign on you.

Write up an operation in which the agent carrying out the operation would need a pretty good cover.

Demo how knowing the enemy makes for a better operation than being ignorant of the enemy.

Also included on the check sheet is TR-L (training routine lie). Again, an interesting course for a church!

Unquestionably, the most spectacular operation carried out by GO agents were those connected to Operation Snow White, in which scores of government offices were burglarized in an attempt to retrieve every government file on Scientology. Those operations resulted in some 30,000 government documents being either copied or stolen. Unfortunately for the Scientologists, they also resulted in the arrest and imprisonment of eleven Scientologists, including Hubbard's wife.

Michael Meisner, as Assistant Guardian for the Bureau of Information, was chosen to supervise the operation. He selected GO staff member Gerald Wolfe to infiltrate the IRS in Washington, DC. Wolfe, codenamed Silver, was hired as a clerk typist with the IRS in May, 1975.

From May, 1975, until June, 1976, Wolfe and Meisner, using Wolfe's ID card as well as five forged cards, burglarized offices of the IRS Chief Counsel, several IRS attorneys, the IRS Exemptions Office, the Tax Division of the US Justice Department, the Deputy General of the US, the IRS Office of Intelligence Operations, the Department of Justice Information and Privacy Unit, and the Interpol Liaison Office.

Meisner and Wolfe were able to pull off their astonishingly successful burglaries for over a year, until a suspicious library clerk alerted the authorities. In June, 1976, Wolfe was caught by the FBI with one of the forged ID cards, for which he was arrested and prosecuted. Meisner managed to evade prosecution for a year, during which time he was held prisoner by the GO, until he escaped and defected to the FBI.

One month after Meisner's defection, the FBI launched surprise raids against the GO offices in Washington, DC, and Los Angeles, seizing thousands of documents, including most of those previously stolen from the government offices.

As a result of the evidence obtained in the raids, eleven GO officials were indicted, and nine of those eleven served prison sentences ranging from six months to five years. Mary Sue Hubbard, as head of the GO, was fined $10,000 and given a five-year prison sentence for her part in the illegal operations. Although she pleaded for leniency, the judge told her:

> "We have a precious
> system of government in the
> United States.... For anyone to
> use those laws, or to seek under
> the guise of those laws, to
> destroy the very foundation of
> the government is totally wrong
> and cannot be condoned by any
> responsible citizen."[141]

Mary Sue Hubbard reported to The Federal Correctional Institution in Lexington, Kentucky, where she served one year of her term before being released. Shortly after her release from prison, she was ousted from her position as head of the Guardian's Office by the new church leaders. Her present whereabouts remain unknown.

The Guardian's Office was renamed the Office of Special Affairs by the new church leadership in the mid-1980s in an effort to shed the GO's tarnished image. Like the tiger unable to change its stripes, OSA is simply the old GO with a new name.

Strange activities for a church?

True, not every church comes with its own information and intelligence agency, illustrated instructions for burglary, espionage training, and its own corps of highly trained secret agents. The siege mentality of the Scientologists, the idea of "us" against "them," helps maintain a high degree of unity within the cult.

The GO was formed to deal with the many real and perceived "enemies" of Scientology. That enemy mentality was born in the paranoid lobes of Hubbard's mind. That mentality makes the GO, now the OSA, the danger it is.

---

[141] Ibid, p. 364

CHAPTER THIRTEEN

Not So Clear in Clearwater—Scientology Takes Over a Town

The Church of Scientology has engaged in a public relations campaign to present itself to the citizens of Clearwater as a legitimate, law-abiding, non profit religious organization while actually operating...in disregard and in violation of civil and criminal laws. The actual conduct of the Church of Scientology adopted and written as corporate policy, includes the following: (1) burglary; (2) larceny; (3) infiltration; (4) smear campaigns; (5) extortion; (6) blackmail; (7) frame-ups; (8) deceptive sales and recruitment policies; (9) deceptive uses of legal releases and bonds; (10) suppression of free speech and association; (11) deviation from acceptable standards of medical practice and educational requirements; (12) use of tax-exempt funds for unlawful purposes; (13) overtly fraudulent policies designed to extract large sums of money from unwitting and uninformed individuals; (14) extortionate and/or improper use of highly personal information fraudulently procured from individuals based on false promises of confidentiality; (15) the use of unlawful and covertly harassive means to prevent individuals who have been defrauded from obtaining legal redress; (16) and the use of overtly fraudulent policies such as the "minister's mock-up" and "religious image check sheet" to present a "religious front" to the public while actually engaged in the business of unlicensed psychotherapy for the purpose of making money.

Final report to the
Clearwater Hearings, 1983

By the autumn of 1975, Hubbard knew that the Sea Org's days at sea were over. The ports of the Caribbean were proving just as unfriendly as those of the Mediterranean. The final straw came when the *Apollo* was ordered from the port of Curacao by the Dutch prime minister, who referred to the *Apollo* as the "ship of fools."

It's also possible that Hubbard, still convalescing from his latest and most serious heart attack, felt the need for a more stable, permanent place to roost.

In October, 1975, the Sea Org came ashore. The crew was divided into groups and traveled as inconspicuously as possible, one to New York, another to Washington, DC, and a third to Miami, where they established "Flag Relay Offices" in the existing orgs. A fourth group took up residence in a motel in Daytona Beach, Florida, while scouts began looking for a suitable property for a "Flag Land Base."

Hubbard, who traveled from the Bahamas with his aides bearing false passports and a million dollars in cash, was temporarily situated in another Daytona motel near his crew.

Scouts soon returned with good tidings. An ideal property was available in Clearwater, a sleepy tourist town on Florida's west coast.

The name *Clear*water would certainly appeal to a Scientologist! A decision was soon made to buy the old Ft. Harrison Hotel in downtown Clearwater.

Representatives of the Southern Land Development and Leasing Corporation, which they said represented the United Churches of Florida, approached the hotel owners and said they wished to buy the property.

The hotel was purchased for $2.3 million in cash, and a nearby bank building was also purchased for $550,000 in cash. When reporters asked who was behind Southern Land Development and United Churches, they were told only that the purchases were made by a property investor who wished to remain anonymous. United Churches was explained as a nonprofit organization dedicated to church unity. It would also sponsor a series of Sunday-morning radio broadcasts by local clergy.

The Sea Org began occupying their new headquarters. Swarms of uniformed Scientologists were suddenly visible on the streets of downtown Clearwater, as they moved between the two buildings with cleaning and painting supplies.

Uneasy suspicion grew regarding the new tenants of the Ft. Harrison Hotel. Clearwater Mayor Gabe Cazares voiced the perplexity many felt when he stated, "I am discomfited by the increasing visibility of security personnel, armed with billy clubs and mace, employed by the United Churches of Florida. I am unable to understand why this degree of security is required by a religious organization."[142]

Meanwhile, two reporters, Bette Orsini of the St. Petersburg *Times* and Mark Sableman of the Clearwater *Sun* began to discover that Southern Land Development and United Churches of Florida didn't exist. Nowhere was there any record of either organization.

Bette Orsini of the St. Petersburg *Times* was the first to make the connection with Scientology. Just as the paper was about to print the truth, a Scientology spokesman from Los Angeles, Arthur Maren, arrived in Clearwater and announced to the press that it was the controversial Church of Scientology that bought the buildings.

At first, he denied that the hotel would become a Scientology center. He said it would be open to all churches for conferences and retreats. However, the next day, he said that if Scientology failed to bring religious harmony to all religions, then the hotel would become a center for Scientologists. A few days later, he admitted that the center would be used exclusively for Scientology training.

After telling the people of Clearwater that Scientologists were nice, friendly people who wanted to fit in with the community, Scientology launched lawsuits against Gabe Cazares and the St. Petersburg *Times*, both of whom responded with countersuits against the church.

Hubbard, meanwhile, was ensconced in a suite of apartments in the nearby town of Dunedin, but not for long. He engaged the services of a local tailor, who happened to be a science-fiction fan. During their conversation, Hubbard revealed his identity, and the tailor spread the news to his wife and friends. Before long,

---

[142] Miller, p. 337

a reporter arrived at Hubbard's door. Panic stricken, he immediately fled with two aides, who drove him to safety in Washington, DC.

The Ft. Harrison Hotel was being advertised as the *Mecca of Technical Perfection* and was becoming a place where well-to-do Scientologists from around the world could come to receive the best that Scientology had to offer.

> The public preclears would fly in from Los Angeles, Zurich, Frankfurt, or Mexico City. They would pay huge fees, play backgammon, swim, sunbathe, and listen to tapes by Hubbard, and be given special PR briefings by a smartly uniformed host or attractive PR girls....
>
> Diners in the Hour Glass Restaurant, which is part of the Ft. Harrison Hotel, were, and are to this day, served by waiters in black suits, bowties, and crisp white shirts. The talk would usually drift to the great wins each was having in his auditing.[143]

The Guardian's Office was also hard at work in Clearwater. Gabe Cazares, who had by then become an official enemy of the "church," was the subject of an extensive investigation referred to by the GO as Operation Taco-Less.

The GO investigation of Cazares is of interest, because it shows to what lengths Scientology will go in investigating anyone they perceive as an enemy.

---

[143] Corydon, p. 122

In the write-up of the operation, the major target was stated as:

> To insure that all
> investigative leads and strings
> left unpulled on Mayor Cazares
> are followed up on to discover
> further data about him which
> when released will ruin his
> political career and
> remove/restrain him as an
> opponent of Scientology....

Some of the steps included in their investigation of Cazares were:

1. Compile a list of all clubs, associations, organizations, etc., which Gabe is or has been a member of or which he publicly supports. Obtain membership lists to these groups.

2. Compile a list of all the people who have written letters in the press in support of Cazares. Investigate any people who show up in both of these lists.

3. Conduct interviews under suitable guise with people at Bedford Air Force Base in Massachusetts to see what can be dug up about Cazares.

4. Obtain property records in El Paso to see which property is owned by Cazares or his wife. Interview the inhabitants of the house to see what can be learned about the Cazares.

5. Locate and investigate all of Cazares' relatives, including Arthur, Joseph, and Edmond Cazares (brothers), and Cora P., Marjorie C., and Soledad A. (sisters). They should be investigated to find any scandal or criminal backgrounds they or their family may have.

6. Investigate any unknown property deals of Gabe or his wife.

7.   Check the backgrounds of Gabe's parents in Mexico and the circumstances of their coming to this country.

8.   Check the name of Gabe's first wife, when and where divorced, and why.

9.   Check grammar and high school records of Gabe.

10.   Check all financial disclosure forms for the disbursement of his campaign funds. Check campaign contributors. Insure that he keeps within the letter of the law regarding contributions.

11.   Obtain a copy of Gabe's military records.

12.   Check political backgrounds and affiliations of all Cazares' campaign staff, looking for people with Commie or heavy leftist backgrounds, or with backgrounds which will discredit Cazares.

13.   Obtain marriage records for the first marriage of Cazares' wife, and also the records of the divorce.

Etc.

Apparently, the GO didn't come up with much as a result of their investigation, so they changed tack. A plan was made to frame Cazares in a hit-and-run accident designed to ruin his political career, which it almost did.

It was known that he planned to attend a Mayor's Conference in Washington, DC. He was met at the airport by a young man posing as a reporter and his female friend. Both were Scientologists. The female, a GO agent named Sharon Thomas, volunteered to show Gabe the sights of the city, and he gladly accepted.

As they drove through Rock Creek Park, Sharon, who was driving, struck a pedestrian, who crumpled to the ground behind the car. It was actually GO agent Michael Meisner, who, of course, wasn't seriously hurt. Sharon drove on without stopping to see if the "pedestrian" was hurt.

Somehow, the event was leaked to the press, and it reached the headlines in Clearwater, costing Cazares his election as a congressional candidate.

The GO also drew up plans to have someone in Mexico forge a document that Cazares had been married in Mexico twenty-five years earlier, making his current marriage bigamous. That operation was apparently never carried out.

The Guardian's Office did manage, however, to seriously disrupt Cazares' political career and to make life quite miserable for him and his wife for several years. His lawsuit against the church was settled out of court in the mid-80s.

The GO was simultaneously involved in a complex series of plans called Operation Goldmine, in which Scientology funds were to be spent taking over the town of Clearwater.

In one part of the plan, called *Power Project 3: Normandy,* the major target was given as:

> To fully investigate the
> Clearwater city and county area
> so we can distinguish our friends
> from our enemies and handle as
> needed.

Some of the steps in the plan were:

1. Locate all local medical societies, clinics, hospitals, etc. Gather the names of the main officials and directors of each. Fully investigate each one and recommend handling.
2. Locate all local intelligence agencies (e.g., police, intelligence, FBI office, etc.). Gather the names of the heads of such. Fully investigate each one. Recommend handling.
3. Locate all local PR firms. Gather the names of the main officials and directors of each. Fully

investigate each one and recommend handling.

4. Locate all local drug firms. Gather the names of officials and directors and fully investigate each. Recommend handling.

5. For each government agency listed below, do the following:

    a. Locate the heads or senior officials in charge.

    b. Investigate each one for enemy connections.

    c. Compile a full report on each one with a time track (a consecutive history of their lives).

    d. To each report add your recommended handling of the person, i.e., "ops" (operation), penetration, keep an eye on him, or he's a potential ally, etc.

Do this in full for the following agencies:

City Council

    City Health Department
    City Mental Hygiene Department
    City Building and Safety Department
    City Police Department
    City Consumer Affairs Office
    City Attorney or Prosecuting Attorney
    County Commissioners
    County Health Department
    County Mental Health Department
    County Building and Safety Department
    County Licensing Department
    County Sheriff
    County Attorney or Prosecutor
    Florida State Attorney's local office
    Board of Medical Examiners
    Florida State Mental Health Department
    Florida State Senators (local)
    Florida State Representative (local)

Local US Congressmen
Local US Senators
1. Locate all local media companies. Gather the names of officials and directors of each, fully investigate and recommend handling.
2. Locate all local psych groups (mental health groups, psychiatric societies, clinics, hospitals, etc.). Gather the names of the main officials and directors of each. Fully investigate each one and recommend handling.
3. Locate all local finance institutions (banks, investment houses, etc.). Gather the names of the main officials and directors of each. Fully investigate each one and recommend handling.

Another part of Operation Goldmine, called *Power Project 4: Tricycle,* goes further. The Major Target of Tricycle states:

> To proof up ourselves against any potential threat by taking control of the key points in the Clearwater area.
>
> Any obstacle or opposition...that arises must be removed to the point of no further threat or barrier to obtaining the Major Target.

Some of the steps in this plan were:

1. List out all news media and the heads or proprietors of news media that are distributed or broadcast in the Clearwater area. Work out a way to gain control or allegiance of each. (Note: Control can mean buying the media or controlling interest in it, or it can mean holding a powerful position with the media.)

2. Locate key political figures (ones who influence the area). Work out a way to get control or allegiance of each.
3. Locate the key financial influences in the community. Work out a way to gain control or allegiance of each.
4. Locate the people or groups peculiar to the Clearwater area which exert the greatest control/influence in the area (possible example: Board of Realtors). Work out a way to gain the control or allegiance of each.
5. Submit all plans to the GO for approval. Implement approved handlings when received.

Operations Goldmine and Tricycle were just two parts of the Operation Goldmine master plan. It's probably safe to assume that there was much more to Goldmine than what is revealed here.

That is the systematic way in which the Guardian's Office in Scientology goes about taking over, or "neutralizing," a city such as Clearwater. The same strategy could be applied to any city, anywhere. By all appearances, Operation Goldmine has successfully achieved its objectives in Clearwater.

In the early 1980s, opposition to the presence of Scientology in Clearwater was loud and vocal. Frequent rallies were held at the city hall behind the hotel, protest marches regularly circled the hotel, lively discussions were aired daily in the Clearwater *Sun* newspaper, cars passing by the hotel honked their horns, creating a real problem for Scientologists trying to audit in the quiet of their rooms.

Today, the situation is different. There's a sense of apathy among the Clearwater residents. Many local businesses have closed or relocated to the suburbs, giving Scientology a more complete occupation of downtown

Clearwater, where the organization owns a large percentage of the land and buildings.

The newspaper most vocally opposed to Scientology has gone out of business. The articles printed in the surviving Clearwater *Times* are cautious and temperate, carefully avoiding anything provocative to the litigious Scientologists.

Scientologists hand out tickets for free personality tests on Clearwater beach. Many Clearwater natives or their children have become involved in Scientology. The public relations campaign waged tirelessly by the church, that Scientology is against drugs, for the rights of the aged, pro-family—any local issue they can find—has been successful.

The position of the community slowly changed from that of angry defiance to a position of powerlessness and grudging acceptance.

A series of hearings on Scientology held in Clearwater in the early 1980s uncovered much interesting sociological information about the cult, but efforts to translate the findings of those hearings into meaningful action have been hampered by bureaucratic red tape and legal problems.

Many people in Clearwater sense something sinister about Scientology, but they admit they know little about the actual beliefs and practices of the cult. They remain puzzled and perplexed by the swarms of uncommunicative, uniformed young people inhabiting their town. It is as if the town has been invaded by aliens.

Clearwater remains an occupied city, one that is under siege, and no one seems to know what to do about it.

CHAPTER FOURTEEN

Brainwashing and Thought Control in Scientology—

The Road to Rondroid

(The techniques used in modern brainwashing) are not like the medieval torture of the rack and the thumbscrew. They are subtler, more prolonged, and intended to be more terrible in their effect. They are calculated to disintegrate the mind of an intelligent victim, to distort his sense of values, to a point where he will not simply cry out, "I did it!" but will become a seemingly willing accomplice to the complete disintegration of his integrity and the production of an elaborate fiction.

Dr. Charles W. Mayo, The Rape of the Mind

In part, the totalitarian state is sustained because individuals terrorize themselves—they become accomplices in their own tyrannization, censoring what they say and even what they allow themselves to think and feel.

Willa Appel, Cults in

America

The effectiveness of a
doctrine does not come from its
meaning but from its certitude....
Crude absurdities, trivial
nonsense, and sublime truths
are equally potent in readying
people for self-sacrifice if they are
accepted as the sole, eternal
truth.... It is obvious, therefore,
that in order to be effective, a
doctrine must not be understood,
but has to be believed in.

Eric Hoffer, The True
Believer

Most people think that brainwashing is something
that happens only in Communist countries like Russia or
North Korea. There's some validity to that belief, because
brainwashing was developed in those countries, where it
was used for psycho-political purposes.

Brainwashing is defined as *the process of causing a
person to undergo a radical alteration of beliefs and
attitudes.... The brainwashed person is conditioned by
punishment for undesirable beliefs and rewarded for
expressing desirable beliefs.*[144]

Ex-cult members and their families are only too aware of
the truth—that brainwashing does exist in America. *An
uncomfortable reality has at last come home to the American
public: brainwashing, which once seemed exclusively a
Communist technique, is here in America and used by cults.*[145]

Hundreds of former cult
members testify this is so in

---

[144] Verdier, p. 11

[145] Ibid, p. 13

court proceedings, public
information hearings concerning
the cults, magazine and
newspaper interviews, and
counseling sessions.
Psychiatrists and other
professionals who counsel former
cultists confirm this....

These techniques include
constant repetition of doctrine,
application of intense peer
pressure, manipulation of diet so
that critical faculties are
adversely affected, deprivation of
sleep, lack of privacy and time for
reflection, complete break with
past life, reduction of outside
stimulation and influences, the
skillful use of ritual to heighten
mystical experience, and the
invention of new vocabulary and
the manipulation of language to
narrow down the range of
experience and construct a new
reality.[146]

Ronald Enroth describes what he calls the "seduction
syndrome." Many of those inducted into a cult like
Scientology come in searching for identity or for spiritual
reality, and this is especially true of young people.

Coming to grips with one's
identity has always been a part of
adolescence in America, but
today's youth face difficulties
compounded by the massive
cultural and social upheavals that

---

[146] Rudin, p. 16

characterize the contemporary
world, especially during the last
decade.... Despite the boom in
entertainment and the pervasive
impact of the mass media, youth
often remain bored, unfulfilled,
and lonely.... The tendency to drift
in and out of jobs, college, and
sexual relationships; uncertainty
and anxiety regarding the future;
discontent with economic and
political structures—all contribute
to isolation and loneliness.[147]

Most cult members had previous experience in a
traditional church or synagogue, however:

Cult seekers have found
these conventional religious
institutions to be lacking in
spiritual depth and meaning,
incapable of inspiring
commitment and providing clear-
cut answers, and often
hypocritical in everyday life.[148]

In contrast, the cults provide black-and-white
answers to the questions of life.

Cults not only provide firm
answers to every question but
also make promises that appeal
to those needing reassurance,
confidence, and affirmation.[149]

---

[147] Enroth, p. 150

[148] Ibid, p. 153

[149] Ibid, p. 153

Many people come into a cult such as Scientology at a time in their lives when they are undergoing unusual stress or crisis. An example of this is the first-year college student, away from home for the first time.

> Other precipitating life experiences that increase vulnerability include such things as a recent divorce of one's parents or a similar serious problem in the home; the extended, critical illness of a family member; a break-up with a girlfriend or boyfriend; poor academic performance or failure; or unpleasant experiences with drugs or sex. When someone is feeling exceedingly anxious, uncertain, hurt, lonely, unloved, confused, or guilty, that person is a prime prospect for those who come in the guise of religion offering a way out or peace of mind.[150]

There are a small minority of people who are drawn to the cult because of chronic emotional problems, often as a result of growing up in a dysfunctional home.

The lonely, unstable, vulnerable—cult recruiters seem to have the ability to spot those people in a crowd. They seem to have a sixth sense for people who will make prime candidates for the cult.

Recruitment of the vulnerable is one element of Enroth's *seduction syndrome.* Other elements include: intense group pressure and group activity, such as that experienced by the newcomer on the introductory course, the Communication Course of Scientology; sensory

---

[150] Ibid, p. 154

deprivation, a lack of proper nutrition and adequate sleep, also experienced by Scientologists, who may be fed a diet of rice and beans as a punishment for inadequate production; and a dramatic change in worldview—the adopting of beliefs radically different from those held before.

In another paradigm of brainwashing, Willa Appel describes a three-stage conversion process, which is also applicable to the Scientologist.

In the first stage of the conversion, the recruit is isolated from his past life.

> First the individual is
> isolated from his past life, cut off
> from his former position and
> occupation, as well as those with
> whom he has emotional ties.[151]

In Scientology, this is accomplished in several ways. In gradually adopting a new language, the recruit to Scientology is subtly separated from those in his past who no longer "speak his language." The use of the term *wog,* a derogatory term, to refer to those outside Scientology, accomplishes the same end. Additionally, the student is pressured to spend every available minute "on course," instead of on frivolous pursuits outside Scientology, which are termed "off purpose."

In the second phase of conversion:

> The loss of name and
> identity is reinforced by inducing
> the novice, emotionally and
> intellectually, to surrender his
> past life. Humiliation and guilt
> are the basic tools in the
> psychological dismembering of

---

[151] Appel, p. 77

the former self.[152]

In Scientology, this phase is accomplished in two ways. First, through the practice of auditing, also called the "confessional," in which the Scientologist, over time, divulges all the secrets of his entire lifetime. Second, through the "ethics" process of writing up one's OWs (overts and withholds), in which he records every wrong deed, real or imagined, committed in this and previous lifetimes. The Scientologist must produce those OWs until the Ethics Officer is satisfied that he is reduced to an acceptable level of contrition and humiliation.

In the third phase of Appel's conversion, the convert assumes a new identity and a new worldview.[153]

In Scientology, this is accomplished through a rigorous process of indoctrination through written and tape-recorded materials. The member's confidence in all previously trusted social institutions is eroded and replaced with the belief that salvation can come only through Scientology. The person's new sense of identity comes from his belonging to the cult, as all other allegiances are severed.

A third paradigm of mind control, or brainwashing, comes from George Estabrooks in his writing about hypnotism, about which he was an expert. He noticed that many of the elements of mob psychology used by cult leaders were very similar to techniques used by hypnotists. He states that those techniques were used by Hitler. They were also practiced by Hubbard.

Of the six essential points in the psychology of the mob, the first is:

> (The cult leader) will strive
> for a restriction of the field of

---

[152] Ibid, p. 77

[153] Ibid, p. 77

consciousness among the
members of his mob (cult).... His
ideas, and his ideas only, are to
be considered by the mob
(cult).... His followers hear only
one line of thought, his line of
thought.[154]

That will sound very familiar to a Scientologist. Scientologists are strictly forbidden against "mixing practices," from studying any other system of thought while in Scientology. Hubbard, as Source, is regarded as ultimate authority and as infallible. Any confusion or disagreement with anything said or written by Hubbard is regarded as a misunderstanding, or a "misunderstood word" on the part of the student.

The second point in mob psychology is that the dictator will appeal to the emotions.... Moreover, he will appeal to the baser emotions of fear, anger, hatred.[155]

In Scientology, there is an appeal to fear and to guilt. The ideology of Scientology is that we are caught in a trap, and that Scientology is the only way out. Fear is also maintained within the group by the office of "ethics," through which any doubts, disagreements, or failures within the group are punished. Members having serious disagreements or difficulties are threatened with expulsion and the label of "Suppressive Person," or eternal condemnation.

Third, the mob (cult) leader will count on emotional contagion, an extremely important factor in all mob (cult) situations.... Emotions are far more contagious than the measles.... Humans tend to fit into the emotional pattern

---

[154] Estabrooks, p. 216

[155] Ibid, p. 216

of a group.[156]

In Scientology, the prevailing emotion is a sense of urgency and fear. Scientologists at work don't walk, they run. Everything is deadly serious and urgent. The world is at stake. Each small victory has added significance. Scientology is a group at war, and that mentality lends fervor, enthusiasm, and a sense of danger to every activity.

Fourth, we have the matter of social sanction. The individual feels justified in any action approved by the mob (cult) and its leaders....[157]

Because Scientologists believe themselves to be fighting for the salvation of mankind, any acts—even if they are illegal—that contribute to that purpose are sanctioned by reason of *the greatest good for the greatest number of dynamics.*

The fifth element of mob psychology has to do with omnipotence, the "I'm right, you're wrong," reaction, which we see in the fanatic. It never occurred to the Nazi, it does not occur to the Communist, that there are two sides to an argument.[158]

Scientology, to the Scientologist, is the only truth. That fact has caused enormous frustration for many family members trying to reason with the Scientologist in their family. The mind of the Scientologist is closed to any possibility other than Scientology. There is no other side to the argument.

Finally, there is the removal of inhibitions. *Anything goes if the party sanctions such activity.*[159] Jonestown was a shocking example of that aspect of the cult mentality.

---

[156] Ibid, p. 217

[157] Ibid, p. 218

[158] Ibid, p. 219

[159] Ibid, p. 220

Scientology is another potential Jonestown, except on a much wider scale.

Robert Lifton identifies eight features common to all forms of what he calls "ideological totalism," eight psychological themes common to an environment in which brainwashing is present:

Milieu control
Mystical manipulation
The demand for purity
The cult of confession
The sacred science
Loading the language
Doctrine over person
The dispensing of existence

Each of those features can be found in Scientology.

In milieu control, the cult controls both the environment and the communication of the cult member. Scientology is a very controlled environment. The existence of the Ethics department provides the threat of punishment for all transgressions against cult norms. Even physical illness is considered the shortcoming of the person and evidence of the existence of "out-ethics."

Communication with those outside Scientology, *wogs,* is manipulated to achieve the cult's desired ends. The cult member's communication with family members, especially those not favorable to the cult, is often dictated by the cult. Communication within the cult follows certain rules. "Upper-level" students may not discuss the contents of those levels even with a spouse. All other Scientologists are forbidden to discuss their "cases" or feelings with other Scientologists. Through the use of "knowledge reports," members critical of the organization may be reported by other members, as in a Communist state.

In "mystical manipulation," the group seeks to inspire in the member certain behaviors and feelings that seem to have originated magically from the environment. In Scientology, the member comes to think and believe just as Hubbard teaches, thinking that such thoughts and beliefs are the result of his own "cognitions," or coming to truth.

With the demand for purity:

...the experiential world is sharply divided into the pure and the impure, into the absolutely good and the absolutely evil. The good and pure are, of course, those feelings and actions which are consistent with the totalist ideology and policy; anything else is apt to be relegated to the bad and the impure.[160]

A good example of this in Scientology is the redefinition of the word *ethics,* which comes to mean that which is good for or benefits Scientology, while anyone against Scientology is an enemy or "SP" (Suppressive Person). A "good" person is one who is most completely aligned with the goals and purposes of Scientology. An "evil" person is one who opposes the "greater good," or Scientology.

The cult of confession is carried out in Scientology through the many levels of auditing, or "confessionals," and through the periodic writing up of one's OWs. That purging oneself of actual and imagined crimes leads to the gradual act of self-surrender to the group. One learns to think only those thoughts sanctioned and acceptable to the group.

The totalist milieu maintains an aura of sacredness around its basic dogma, holding it out as an ultimate moral vision for the ordering of human existence.[161]

That is what Lifton calls "sacred science."

---

[160] Lifton, p. 423

[161] Ibid, p. 427

Scientology to a Scientologist is absolute truth, and there is a certain comfort in that belief. Having black-and-white answers to the complex questions of life shields one from the insecurity and uncertainty of ambiguity, and it's one of the great attractions of Scientology for its members.

Hubbard, a persuasive and dynamic speaker, made many claims about the scientific validity of his science, none of which have ever been subjected to the rigors of the scientific method but which are accepted at face value by his trusting disciples.

The language of the totalist environment is characterized by the thought-terminating cliché.... (it is) the language of nonthought.[162]

Scientologists have their own dictionary. A conversation between two Scientologists might not make sense to a non-Scientologist. Lifton states:

The effect of the language of ideological totalism can be summed up in one word: constriction. He is, so to speak, linguistically deprived; and since language is so central to all human experience, his capacities for thinking and feeling are immensely narrowed.[163]

An example of that kind of constriction of thought is the phrase in Scientologese, "My 2-D and I are in ARC," which can be translated as, "The person I am romantically involved with, either as a lover or a spouse, and I have a great deal of love for each other. We share basically the same beliefs. We communicate well with each other. There is a shared understanding between us that is very positive."

---

[162] Ibid, p. 429

[163] Ibid, p. 430

Other examples of loaded language are the words "reality," "ethics," and "suppressive," the latter containing a world of meaning for a Scientologist.

Lifton also describes the primacy of doctrine over person:

...the demand that character and identity be reshaped, not in accordance with one's special nature or potentialities, but rather to fit the rigid contours of the doctrinal mold.[164]

A Scientologist is never allowed to think about the "tech" or the "science" developed by Hubbard. To alter the tech in any way is denounced as "squirreling," for which crime one can be expelled from Scientology. Questioning the doctrine is forbidden. Doubts or questions are euphemistically relabeled as MUs, or misunderstood words on the part of the student.

The totalist environment draws a sharp line between those whose right to existence can be recognized, and those who possess no such right...known as nonpeople.[165]

In Scientology, there are two types of "nonpeople"— wogs and SPs. Wogs are those who have yet to become enlightened as to Scientology. SPs, or suppressive persons, have no right to exist, and that is declared by Scientology's "Fair Game Law," which states that enemies of Scientology can be "sued, tricked, lied to, or destroyed." That is the dispensing of existence within Scientology.

One of the phenomena common to many cults is the personality change in the cult member after conversion. That has been a frightening change for many families. Sometimes, the change occurs gradually, but, in other cases, it occurs in a single experience, called "snapping"

---

[164] Ibid, p. 431

[165] Ibid, p. 433

by one team of researchers.[166] The cult personality is radically different from the precult personality.

There is evidence that the change is organic as well as psychological. Exposing a person to a radical change in environment and an overload of new, radically different information may actually cause a change in the neurotransmitters in the brain. The substances norepinephrine and serotonin in the brain have similar chemical compositions as mescaline or LSD. When sensory flow to the brain becomes severely restricted or suddenly overloaded, it can trigger a state of increased suggestibility or the symptoms of dissociation or hallucinations.

In Scientology, that can occur in the hypnotic practice of TR-0, or during the long hours on Scientology courses.

Psychiatrist Dr. John Clark of Harvard University believes that the cults, including Scientology, are psychologically dangerous:

In cults, people are presented with stressful circumstances, especially huge loads of new information, at times in their lives when they are vulnerable, and they dissociate. What the...Scientologists and all the other dangerous cults do is maintain the dissociation. They keep the parts of the mind—the connections inside the central nervous system—divided in function, in action, and in their connection with the outer world. It's a way of controlling them, and, the longer it goes on, the further apart all of this gets to be—like the chronic schizophrenic.[167]

Did Hubbard really believe in Scientology, or was he just a calculating conman?

---

[166] Conway & Siegelman, p.13

[167] Appel, p. 134

Estabrooks describes what he calls the "sincere dictator:"

> The dictator may be, and
> generally is, a man of great
> personal courage. He plays along
> grimly till the last throw of the
> dice and meets his fate with his
> chin up. This may be because he
> is perfectly sincere. This sounds
> like a strange contradiction, but
> we must accept it. The dictator
> really believes that he is God's
> chosen instrument—or society's
> chosen instrument, if he does not
> believe in God—to lead his group,
> or possibly the entire world, into
> the promised land. The resulting
> picture is not pleasant, and the
> individual who creates that
> picture is easily the most
> dangerous of all the mentally
> maladjusted. He has intelligence,
> conviction, drive, courage, and
> will be utterly unscrupulous—a
> combination which calls for
> serious concern.[168]

Those who knew him will agree that that is a fair description of Hubbard.

One important clue to Hubbard's motivations lies in a book he wrote in the midfifties, called *Brainwashing Manual*. Although there were witnesses that he wrote the book, he attributed authorship to the infamous Russian politician Beria, then pretended to "discover" it.

Some passages of the book reveal much about Hubbard:

---

[168] Estabrooks, p. 223

It is not enough for the State (Scientology) to have goals.

These goals, once put forward, depend for their completion upon the loyalty and obedience of the workers (Scientologists). These engaged for the most part in hard labors, have little time for idle speculation, which is good....

Hypnosis is induced by acute fear.... Belief is engendered by a certain amount of fear and terror from an authoritative level, and this will be followed by obedience.

The body is less able to resist a stimulus if it has insufficient food and is weary.... Refusal to let them sleep over many days, denying them adequate food, then brings about an optimum state for the receipt of a stimulus.

Degradation and conquest are companions.

By lowering the endurance of the person...and by constant degradation and defamation, it is possible to induce, thus, a state of shock which will receive adequately any command given.

Any organization which has the spirit and courage to display inhumanity, savageness, brutality...will be obeyed. Such a use of force is, itself, the essential ingredient of greatness.

And:

> In rearranging loyalties, we must have command of their values. In the animal, the first loyalty is to himself. This is destroyed by demonstrating errors in him...the second loyalty is to his family unit.... This is destroyed by lessening the value of marriage, by making an easiness of divorce, and by raising the children whenever possible by the State. The next loyalty is to his friends and local environment. This is destroyed by lowering his trust and bringing about reportings upon him allegedly by his fellows or the town or village authorities. The next loyalty is to the State (Church of Scientology) and this, for the purposes of Communism (Scientology), is the only loyalty which should exist.

And finally:

> The tenets of rugged individualism, personal determinism, self-will, imagination, and personal creativeness are alike in the masses antipathetic to the good of the Greater State (Scientology). These willful and unaligned are no more than illnesses which will bring about disaffection, disunity, and, at length, the collapse of the group to which the individual is attached.

> The constitution of man
> lends itself easily and thoroughly
> to certain and positive regulation
> from without of all of its
> functions, including those of
> thinkingness, obedience, and
> loyalty, and these things must be
> controlled if the Greater State
> (Scientology) is to ensue.

> The end thoroughly
> justifies the means.[169]

Did Hubbard know what he was doing? The answer is yes. Driven by greed, by his twin lusts for money and power, he willfully and knowingly destroyed the lives of the thousands naïve enough to follow him.

L. Ron Hubbard—pied piper of the soul.

---

[169] Corydon, p. 107-9

CHAPTER FIFTEEN

Conclusion—Coming Out of Scientology: The Nightmare Ends, the Nightmare Begins

> For weeks after I left, I would suddenly feel spacey and hear the cult leader saying, "You'll always come back. You are one with us. You can never separate."
>
> I'd forget where I was. I got so frightened once that I slapped my face to make it stop.

Ex-cult member quoted in *Prison or Paradise*

> The last time I ever witnessed a movement that had these qualifications: (1) a totally monolithic movement with a single point of view and a single authoritarian head; (2) replete with fanatical followers who are prepared and programmed to do anything their master says; (3) supplied by absolutely unlimited funds; (4) with a hatred of everyone on the outside; (5) with suspicion of parents, against their parents—the last movement that had those qualifications was the Nazi youth movement, and I'll tell you, I'm scared.

Rabbi Maurice Davis, *Youth, Brainwashing, and the Extremist Cults*

For me, by far the most difficult part of my Scientology experience was in leaving the cult. Being a Scientologist wasn't always easy—the work was hard, the hours long, and the pay almost nonexistent. For the most part, we had to be satisfied with the intangible rewards of knowing we were helping rescue the planet and save mankind.

There were some good things about being a Scientologist. One had the pleasure of working with a group of similarly committed friends toward a goal that seems worthwhile. There was always plenty to do, and one had the satisfaction of working hard and completing challenging tasks. Because of the communal lifestyle, there were always people to be with and talk to. In Scientology, as in many cults, it's hard to be lonely.

I worked at many different jobs in the organization over a twelve-year period. I traveled up the "Grade Chart" through the various Scientology Levels and completed three of the secret "upper" or "OT Levels," to a point where I was supposed to have regained some of my magical, long lost "OT abilities," such as the ability to travel outside my body at will and to be "at cause" over physical objects.

My personal demise within Scientology came at the exact point that I began to utter the one thing a good Scientologist must never say, a simple, three-word phrase that is guaranteed to get one excommunicated from Scientology—"It doesn't work."

I was at the Ft. Harrison Hotel in Clearwater, Florida, Scientology's "Mecca of Technical Perfection," where celebrities and the well-to-do from home and abroad casually write out $100,000 checks as they pursue the elusive promises of "the Tech."

My auditing, paid for by a $16,000 inheritance from my grandmother, wasn't going well. Nothing was happening. Where were the magical "gains" I'd been promised?

I became a problem, a liability, to the organization. I was complaining a bit too publicly. The emperor had no clothes, but, as long as no one said so, the game could continue. I was spoiling the fun.

For several weeks, I was confined to a room on the hotel's second floor. Meals were brought to me. One evening, I was told to pack. The next morning, I was escorted to the Tampa airport, where I was told to choose anyplace outside the state of Florida and go there with a one-way ticket.

I was in shock, because I knew what it meant. I was being "offloaded," Scientology's form of exile. I was no longer welcome in Scientology, which had been my world for twelve years.

I flew back to Wisconsin, where my parents now lived. My father met me at the airport. Soon, I sat in the living room of my parents' home, staring at the snow drifting outside the window, trying to assemble my fractured sense of reality into some kind of coherent, workable mental order.

For the first week, all I could do was work on a huge jigsaw puzzle of the Neuschwanstein Castle in Germany. Slowly fitting the pieces together seemed to correspond to an internal process taking place in my mind. I was still unable to think.

I noticed that when my father turned on the TV, there were periods of time when I stared at the screen, yet the announcer's words were in a foreign language. I knew that was strange, because my father understood it just fine.

My relationship to reality was tenuous for a long time. I had periods of "floating," when I experienced a strange feeling of being disconnected from everything around me and I felt blissfully apart from it all.

The bliss was short-lived. Feelings of terror soon emerged, as I began to deal with my predicament. I'd been exiled from Scientology and would probably be declared an SP, Suppressive Person, a death sentence not only for the current lifetime but for trillions of years to come. It was a scary thought.

For the first few weeks, I couldn't go anywhere by myself. I felt too fragile. Even walking around the block alone became a major challenge. The sudden, unexpected rejection by the cult caused a complete loss of psychic cohesion that took months to rebuild. I was, to be blunt, a "basket case."

Even though I'd been a computer programmer while in the cult, the only work I could do now was as a waitress, because it didn't require any complex thought. The physical work was actually therapeutic. Concentrating on menial tasks helped pull my mind back together.

It wasn't until eighteen months later that I went through my post-cult "crisis." I began feeling an unfamiliar emotion boiling up inside me—anger. I had given them everything for twelve years, my time, energy, any money I had, and my inheritance. How could they just throw me out?

The more the anger brewed, the more I was forced to seek an outlet. I began having dangerous thoughts, suppressive thoughts. One night, I picked up the phone and called a lawyer I knew who was anti-Scientology. It was a clearly suppressive act, and I was terrified.

He asked me some questions and promised to send me some information to read. The knowledge that I had committed a suppressive act threw me into a suicidal crisis. I was tormented with guilt for what I'd done.

I got in my father's car and drove through town, trying to decide what to do. Finally, I stopped at a phone booth and looked through the yellow pages. I called the local hospital and explained to the person who answered that I was in trouble.

A man gave me directions to the hospital. I was surprised to find that he was a priest. He took me to a cafeteria and asked me questions about Scientology. Later, he took me to the house of a couple who had a son in the Moonies. I stayed there for the weekend, and, with their help, began to recover my balance.

After that, I made progress. I read books about other cults, thinking maybe that wasn't quite as suppressive as reading anti-Scientology books. Seeing the similarities between other cults and Scientology was what finally helped snap me out of Scientology.

I visited a religious bookstore to seek books about cults and happened to pick up one about Christianity, which was my religion before the cult. One night, while reading all those books, I was struck by a startling realization. All those cult leaders said they were God, but there could be only one God. Which one was it?

In an instant, I realized Hubbard wasn't God. Simultaneously, I experienced something miraculous. I snapped out of Scientology. I jolted awake, as if an invisible hypnotist had snapped his fingers, and a light went on in my mind.

Hubbard was wrong. Scientology was wrong. I was free. That was my turning point.

Soon after that, I returned to Florida to begin my long legal battle with the cult. I had to do something to channel the anger I felt toward them, or that anger would destroy me.

People don't understand how long it takes to recover from the experience of a destructive cult. Just as veterans from a battlefield go through an extended period of post-traumatic stress disorder, so do refugees from a cult.

It's ironic that I spent twelve years in the cult, and it took me another twelve to fully recover from the experience. It was an expensive lesson.

Margaret Singer, of the American Family Foundation, and others have written about some of the problems facing a former cult member. I will relate them to my own experience.

The one shared by almost all former members of any cult is depression. There's a loss of friends left behind, years wasted, and the loss of innocence and self-esteem. Dr. John Clark of Harvard University writes:

> A person who comes out of
> a cult has been plunged into a
> grief state. He has lost
> something, and it can't be
> returned. These feelings must be
> dealt with by the therapist as
> though he were dealing with the
> real elements of grief. There is a
> real loss. Something has died.
> The person cannot go back. He
> has a right to grieve and
> mourn.[170]

Another big problem for many former cult members is loneliness. During my twelve years in Scientology, I was hardly ever alone. The loneliness I felt when I was out of the cult was devastating. The cult provides a natural support network that can be acquired only with time and effort outside the cult.

Margaret Singer writes:

> Leaving a cult also means
> leaving many friends, a
> brotherhood with common
> interests, and the intimacy of

---

[170] Appel, p. 158

sharing a very significant
experience. It means having to
look for new friends in an
uncomprehending or suspicious
world.[171]

Another problem that was difficult for me was making decisions, especially small ones. What to order from a menu? What to wear? What to do with free time? Which station to watch on TV? Which way to go when taking a walk?

Many times, I feared to make a decision thinking I'd make the wrong one, even when there wasn't a "wrong" decision.

Learning to waste time is still a problem for me after living for so many years in the time-structured world of Scientology, where we had to graph our production every hour of the day. It's still hard for me to waste time, watch TV, read a book for pleasure, go to the mall, or see a movie. There's still a feeling of guilt, though it's diminishing with time.

Trying not to think or speak in Scientologese was another hurdle in recovery. There are still some words that have no suitable English equivalent, like *ARC break,* or *comm lag.* Occasionally, I revert to a word in the cult language, but that habit also seems to be diminishing with time.

My confidence was shaken by my experience with Scientology. If I could be that wrong once, why couldn't it happen again? I'm much more conservative in my beliefs than when I was in the cult, and much less likely to share them with others.

---

[171] Article by Dr. Margaret Singer, *Coming Out of the Cults,* in

Psychology Today, January, 1979, p. 76

Scientology threatened my life when I first decided to initiate a lawsuit, and there's always the fear of retribution. I can't take my personal safety for granted, and I frequently have nightmares about the cult.

It's very hard to explain my experience in the cult to people who ask things like, "You're so smart. How could you ever have gotten involved with a group like that?" Trying to explain the complexities of mind control in Scientology to someone who has no equivalent experience is difficult, if not impossible.

I had to deal with guilt feelings after I discovered that Scientology was wrong, because while in the cult, I persuaded several others to become involved, including one who signed a billion-year contract to work for the Sea Org.

There were other problems. When I came out of Scientology, I was twelve years behind my peers in terms of finance and career. I had the equivalent of a PhD in Scientology. After I snapped out of Scientology, I burned all my Scientology certificates. Starting over in school with much younger classmates intensified my feelings of alienation and failure.

There's also the syndrome of being "elite no more." In Scientology, as in many other cults, we believed we were the elite of the planet. Coming back to reality was a humbling experience. I had also believed in Scientology that I'd be immune from diseases and from normal death. I believed that on the OT Levels, I'd gain the ability to leave my body at will at death. Becoming an ordinary, vulnerable, mortal human being was also an adjustment.

There is also the dilemma of what to put on job resumés for the years I spent in the cult. It's not something one can tell a prospective employer.

When I snapped out of Scientology, my problems were by no means over. I had to deal with a tremendous amount of anger toward the cult. I also found that in many ways, I was emotionally where I'd been when I joined the cult. All those adolescent problems were right where they'd been twelve years earlier—family and identity problems. Emotionally, the years I spent in the cult were a time of arrested growth.

Most cult members face a spiritual and ideological void when exiting the cult. The cult provided answers for a great many questions. After as spiritually intense an experience as Scientology, it becomes necessary to fill the void with something else, a process that takes time.

What made the recovery from my cult experience the hardest was the fact that so few people, especially professionals, were able to understand what I was going through. I'm sure it's similar to the feelings of a veteran returning from Vietnam or someone who has been raped. The people who were best able to understand and be supportive were other former cult members.

When I first came out of Scientology, I thought it was an experience I'd never be able to live with. I thought my life had been irreparably destroyed. The real victory for me now is that my experience with Scientology has become an integrated part of my life. It no longer dominates my life or thinking. It's become an accepted part of my past.

There are other victories. Sometimes, when I'm in the bookstore in the mall, I see someone pick up a copy of the Dianetics book. I go up to them and say, "You don't want to read that. It's about Scientology, a destructive and satanic cult. I know. I was in it for twelve years. I don't want you going through the nightmare I went through."

Usually, they're happy for the advice and put the book back on the shelf. In the few cases where they don't, I see them walk out of the store with the book, and I know that just as my nightmare ends, theirs is about to begin.

The greatest victory for me is that no matter how tough life gets or what kind of battles I have to fight, I know it could always be worse.

I could still be in Scientology.

BIBLIOGRAPHY

Appel, Willa. 1983. *Cults in America: Programmed for Paradise.* New York: Holt, Rinehart, and Winston.

Atack, Jon. 1990. *A Piece of Blue Sky.* Secaucus, NJ: Carol Publishing Group.

Burrell, Maurice. 1982. *The Challenge of the Cults.* Grand Rapids, Michigan: Baker Book House.

Conway, Flo, and Siegelman, Jim. 1978. *Snapping: America's Epidemic of Sudden Personality Change.* Philadelphia and New York: JB Lippincott Company.

Cooper, Paulette. 1971. *The Scandal of Scientology.* New York: Tower Publications, Incorporated.

Corydon, Bent. 1987. *L. Ron Hubbard: Messiah or Madman.* Secaucus, NJ: Lyle Stuart.

Enroth, Ronald. 1977. *Youth, Brainwashing, and the Extremist Cults.* Grand Rapids, Michigan: Zondervan Publishing House.

Estabrooks, G. H. 1943. *Hypnotism.* New York: EP Dutton.

Heller, R. K. 1982. *Deprogramming for Do-It-Yourselfers.* Medina, Ohio: The Gentle Press.

Hoffer, Eric. 1951. *The True Believer: Thoughts on the Nature of Mass Movements.* New York: Harper Publishers.

Hyde, Douglas. 1966. *Dedication and Leadership.* Notre Dame, Indiana: University of Notre Dame Press.

Jacobsen, Jeff. 1990. *From Out of the Blue? Debunking a Dianetics Claim.* Unpublished article.

Kaufman, Robert. 1972. *Inside Scientology: How I Joined Scientology and Became Superhuman.* New York: Olympia Press.

King, Francis. 1970. *Ritual Magic in England.* London: Neville Spearman, Limited.

Lamont, Stewart. 1986. *Religion, Inc.: The Church of Scientology.* London: Harrap, Limited.

Lifton, Robert J. 1961. *Thought Reform and the Psychology of Totalism.* New York: W. W. Norton & Company, Incorporated.

Malko, George. 1970. *Scientology: The Now Religion.* New York: Delacorte Press.

Meerloo, Joost, MD. 1956. *The Rape of the Mind: The Psychology of Thought Control, Menticide, and Brainwashing.* Cleveland and New York: The World Publishing Company.

Miller, Russell. 1987. *Bare-Faced Messiah: The True Story of L. Ron Hubbard.* London: Penguin Books, Limited.

Pignotti, Monica. *My Nine Lives in Scientology.* Unpublished manuscript.

Rudin, Marcia and James. 1980. *Prison or Paradise: The New Religious Cults.* Philadelphia: Fortress Press.

Sargent, William. 1957. *Battle for the Mind.* Westport, Connecticut: Greenwood Press.

Schwartz, Ford. *Stage One: The Communication Course.* Unpublished article.

Verdier, Paul A. 1977. *Brainwashing and the Cults.* Los Angeles: Wilshire Book Company.

This organization clearly is schizophrenic and paranoid, and this bizarre combination seems to be a reflection of its founder, L. Ron Hubbard.

Judge Breckenridge, US

Scientology is both immoral and socially obnoxious...it is corrupt, sinister, and dangerous. It is corrupt, because it is based upon lies and deceit and has as its real objective money and power for Mr. Hubbard.... It is sinister, because it indulges in infamous practices both to its adherents, who do not toe the line unquestioningly and to those who criticize or oppose it. It is dangerous, because it is out to capture people, and to indoctrinate and brainwash them so that they become the unquestioning captives and tools of the cult, withdrawn from ordinary thoughts, living, and relationships with others.

Justice Latey, ruling in the High Court of London, 1984

The Government is satisfied...that Scientology is socially harmful. It alienates members of families from each other and attributes squalid and disgraceful motives to all who oppose it; its authoritarian principles and practice are a potential menace to the personality and well-being of those so deluded as to become its followers; above all, its methods can be a serious danger to the health of those who submit to them....

There is no power under existing law to prohibit the practice of Scientology; but the Government has concluded that it is so objectionable that it would be right to take all steps within its power to curb its growth.

Kenneth Robinson, British Minister of Health

Scientology is evil; its techniques evil; its practice a serious threat to the community, medically, morally, and socially; and its adherents are sadly deluded and often mentally ill.... (Scientology is...) the world's largest organization of unqualified persons engaged in the practice of dangerous techniques which masquerade as mental therapy.

Justice Andersen, Supreme Court of Victoria, Australia

Incredulity of our data and validity. This is our finest asset and gives us more protection than any other single asset. If certain parties thought we were real, we would have infinitely more trouble.... Without a public incredulity, we never would have gotten as far as we have. And now it's too late to be stopped. The protection was accidental, but it serves us very well indeed. Remember that next time the ignorant scoff.

L. Ron Hubbard, The Scandal of Scientology

Falsehood must become exposed by truth—and truth, though fought, always in the end prevails.

L. Ron Hubbard, *My Philosophy,* 1965

Margery Wakefield lives in Denver, Colorado, where she works as a caregiver.

She can be reached at:
PO Box 100932
Denver, Colorado 80250

2324105R10160

Printed in Great Britain
by Amazon.co.uk, Ltd.,
Marston Gate.